Expanded & Revised Second Edition

DESPERATE PEOPLE

SERMONS FOR TIMES LIKE THESE

Ann F. Lightner-Fuller

**Little Sally Walker
Ministries**
Towson, *MD*

Desperate People, 2nd Edition: Sermons for Times Like These.
Copyright © 1996, 2004 by Ann F. Lightner-Fuller

Published by
Little Sally Walker Ministries
P.O. Box 20416
Towson, MD 21284-0416

Unless otherwise indicated, all Scripture quotations are taken from the King James Version (KJV) of *The Holy Bible.*

Library of Congress Cataloging-in-Publication Data

A CIP catalogue record for this book is available from the Library of Congress.

Library of Congress Control Number: 200405876

ISBN 0-9741114-1-4

Printed in the United States of America on acid-free paper
10 9 8 7 6 5 4 3 2

Dedication

It is with humble pride that I dedicate this work to:

*the devoted men and women of the
Mt. Calvary African Methodist Episcopal
Church in Towson, Maryland – you have
been my preaching inspiration;*

*my husband, The Rev. Dr. Stanley Fuller,
my son, Lawrence, and my grandson,
Eric—the men who see me through my
desperate times;*

*my daughters, Katrina and Justina, my
daughter-in-law, Vickie, and my grand-
daughters, Aliyah and Lawren—the
young women who make the desperate
times bearable.*

To God be the glory for entrusting me with the gifts
of preaching and teaching.

ACKNOWLEDGMENTS

This new and expanded edition of *DESPERATE PEOPLE* would not have been possible without a lot of support and a lot of love. I am grateful for the ministers who helped to write summary questions to follow the 17 chapters: *Minister Marilyn Aklin, Reverend Lori Hines, Minister Amy Sykes*, and *Minister Charisse Woods*. To my current *Ministers-in-Training* and the nearly 30 daughters and sons, I have prepared for the ministry, thank you for providing the inspiration for many of the new sermons in this book. I have also been moved by the thousands of local and national requests for reprinting this book whenever I have conducted workshops, attended conferences, or preached many of the sermons in this book.

To each of the *Little Sally Walker Ministries'* publication team members who has worked so diligently to get all of my books out—*Lynette Smothers, Natalie Watson, and Dr. Gloria D. Gibson*—thank you for your enthusiasm and encouragement.

Finally, I am blessed with continued spiritual support and guidance from two nationally known bishops in the African Methodist Episcopal Church—*Bishop John R. Bryant* and *Bishop Vashti Murphy McKenzie*. I thank *Bishop Bryant*, my father in ministry, for his contribution to this work and my entire ministry. To *Bishop McKenzie* whose examples continue to compel me to seek excellence...I would also like to say, a sincere thank you! *To God be the Glory*!

FOREWORD

DESPERATE PEOPLE is a wonderful collection of sermons that ought to find its way into the library of every Christian. Certainly, all Christians, both clergy and lay, at one time or the other, have found themselves in desperate situations.

The Rev. Dr. Ann F. Lightner-Fuller is one of America's great preachers. Not only are her sermons full of passion, they are also full of information and inspiration. She always goes to the source! *The Holy Bible* is the world's greatest "How To" book. The gospel is full of instructions on how to live a productive and positive life. Dr. Lightner-Fuller creatively and always dynamically taps into this aspect of our faith.

Repeatedly her sermons remind us that when we find ourselves in a desperate situation, we *can* overcome. Not only does she preach that we can overcome, more importantly, Dr. Lightner-Fuller tells us *how* to overcome! As she so accurately states: *Desperate times do not have to produce desperate people.*

This work is important because it can be used for church-wide institutes or small bible study groups. I would also recommend it for your personal devotional times. You will find helpful questions after each message in *Desperate People* and space for writing your own important insights about your Christian walk.

Take the time to reflect on the questions that reinforce the main theme in each of these spirit-filled sermons.

When we consider the mountain of challenges that we face daily—racism, sexism, mental and physical illnesses, violence, poverty, relationship and spiritual growth issues—it is good to be reminded that God's word provides a way *out* and a way *up*.

Dr. Ann Lightner-Fuller, in this volume, does a masterly job in describing those ways!

Bishop John Richard Bryant
Presiding Prelate, Fifth Episcopal District
African Methodist Episcopal Church

2004

PREFACE

In the year 2003 as I was on my way back to Baltimore, Maryland from a week-long preaching visit to South Africa, I suddenly became aware that God wanted me to produce a second edition of **DESPERATE PEOPLE.** Instead of publishing two new books as I had planned for 2004, I heard God telling me to do otherwise.

He had shown me that people were desperate everywhere. The women of South Africa have the same problems as those in this country; I found they were praying desperately during their desperate times. I could not ignore that life's difficult times had not gone away since **DESPERATE PEOPLE** was first published nearly ten years ago. Then as now, we need encouragement; we need direction, and, most of all, we need God's holy word.

The conditions that produced uncertainty a decade ago—war, poverty, chronic illnesses, inequities in health, neighborhoods, and communities, worsening relationships in families, on the job, and in churches—are still present. As a pastor, I remain convinced that desperate people need spiritual encouragement, divine intervention, and most of all, a personal relationship with an omnipresent, omniscient, and omnipotent God.

It is that relationship that ties the seventeen sermonic themes together in this new and revised edition of **DESPERATE PEOPLE.** While the focus remains on how to handle tough times, what is different is that readers are now challenged to answer two specific questions about their own desperate situations: *Are you moving away from God? Or, are you moving towards God during difficult times?*

What is significant about both queries is that regardless of how you answer, you are going to give a testimony about the role of *faith* in your life. Just because I am a pastor does not mean that I am exempt from *desperate* times. I know all about them; my faith is constantly being tested! Indeed I would not be able to authentically talk about desperate times, if I do not or have not experienced them myself.

As a young girl growing up in the projects of segregated Raleigh, North Carolina, I knew *desperation*. As a young mother who accepted the divine call in 1981 to preach the Word of God, I knew *desperation*. After more than twenty-two years in the ministry, I know *desperation*. I know what it means to have people question whether women should be in the pulpit or hold leadership positions in the church.

But I also know what to do when I am overwhelmed with grief about what is happening in my own family, my neighborhood, my community, my church, and country. I speak from experience as I share my faith and many scriptural answers with you in these sermons.

The Word of God is truly a lamp unto our feet and a light unto our path. There is power in the Word because the Word of God is the same – it never changes! My prayer for you is that this revised and expanded edition of **DESPERATE PEOPLE: SERMONS FOR TIMES LIKE THESE** will make you want to dig deeper into the Word of God.

I pray that you will read with your Bible in hand. I pray that you read the sermonic Scriptures more than once; I challenge you to memorize some of them. Additionally, I encourage you to reflect on the questions at the end of each chapter. For the answers are tantamount to you own your personal testimonies about how God has worked in your life. This edition is also new because the number of sermons has been increased from eight to seventeen. Please read the chapters and follow-up questions more than once. I promise you that you will get something differently out of them, each time you read them again.

I pray also that these messages will help you during troubled times and comfort you or someone you know. The good news is that God is good, all the time! *DESPERATE PEOPLE* is organized to help you share God's goodness via your own personal testimonies about how you got over; how you have overcome *desperate times.*

Whether you read the messages and study questions to yourself or in your bible study groups, during teatime discussion sessions or daily devotional readings, I know you will be blessed, indeed!

The *Table of Contents*, alone, will assist you in finding answers to serious questions about desperate times. Regardless of the theme in each chapter, God has a Word for helping you *up and out* of your situation. Read the chapters and the questions out loud, alone or in a group—the *Living Word* is meant to be heard!

It's good to have the Word to fall back on during these desperate times, isn't it? I know what it means to be unsaved and saved; to live without salvation and to live with it. I pray that you also know the difference! May the peace of God be with you and yours! May you come to know the extent to which God really does have blessings with your name on them.

Ann Farrar Lightner-Fuller
Towson, MD

God is our refuge and strength, a very present help in trouble.

—Psalm 46

CONTENTS

CONTENTS

DESPERATE PEOPLE

Sermons for Times Like These

The LORD is my shepherd;
I shall not want.

—Psalm 23

CHAPTER I

DON'T LET THE NIGHT BEAT YOU

St. Luke 24:1-9

Now upon the first *day* of the week, very early in the morning, they came unto the sepulchre, bringing the spices which they had prepared, and certain *others* with them. 2 And they found the stone rolled away from the sepulchre. 3 And they entered in, and found not the body of the Lord Jesus. 4 And it came to pass, as they were much perplexed thereabout, behold, two men stood by them in shining garments: 5 And as they were afraid, and bowed down *their* faces to the earth, they said unto them, Why seek ye the living among the dead? 6 He is not here, but is risen: remember how he spake unto you when he was yet in Galilee, 7 Saying, *The Son of Man must be delivered into the hands of sinful men, and be crucified, and the third day rise again.* 8 And they remembered his words, 9 And returned from the sepulchre, and returned from the sepulchre, and told all these things unto the eleven, and to all the rest.

Have you ever noticed that *desperate people* do desperate things in the night? Night is not only symbolic of darkness but the absence of light is often, for many, a time of hopelessness, and a time of despair. Even though the sun is shining ever so brightly, for many it's like nighttime because their hearts are aching. No one seems to care. It's like night when you are lonely and depressed and no one seems to notice your inward pain. It's feels like night when a loved one dies and you are left asking, "WHY?"

So night is not just the hours between six in the evening and five the next morning. When you are going through a *dark night of the soul*, it can be high noon for everyone else, but midnight for you. Jesus knew first hand about darkness and night. It had to be a dark night for Jesus when he announced to his closest disciples that the son of man had to be handed over into the hands of sinful men and crucified. It was a dark night in the garden of Gethsemane when his disciples went to sleep rather than pray with him for one hour, while he agonized over the most important decision of his life.

It was a dark night for Jesus when Judas betrayed him for thirty pieces of silver and turned him over to the Roman soldiers with a kiss on the cheek. It was a dark night when his disciples fled from the garden as the Roman soldiers took him to a mock courtroom.

Jesus was in the darkness of night when Peter, the one who had earlier declared, *I'll never leave you Lord*, denied him not once, but three times before the cock crowed. And let me say that there were no cocks and hens in the Holy City. The hour of 3AM was called cock-crow. Actually a trumpet call was made. The Latin word for trumpet call is *gallicinium* which means "cock-crow." Jesus was in the darkness of night when Pilot said, *I wash my hands of the matter, do with him what you will.* It was night also when the crowd cried out: *Give us Barnabas and crucify Jesus!*

It was night when Jesus endured the cruelest of whippings by Roman Soldiers. And it was the darkest of midnights when they publicly nailed his hands and feet to an old rugged cross before he carried it up Golgotha's hill. It was night when they stood around the cross and hurled cruel remarks at him. They said: *If you are the King of the Jews, come down from the cross.* And when they placed a crown of thorns on his tender head and blood ran down his face; when they spit on him and gambled for his clothes at his feet, it was night.

It was night when a common malefactor said: *If you are the Christ, save yourself and save us too.* My God, it was night when Jesus looked down from the cross and saw tears flowing from his mother's eyes. It was night when he saw John the beloved disciple—the only one who had not deserted him—standing there in sheer agony. Certainly, the last Thursday and

Friday of Jesus' life was engulfed with the darkest of nights imaginable!

Jesus experienced the true meaning of night—not simply the dark hours when we usually sleep and refresh our tired bodies. But a night that symbolized pain, a night that symbolized suffering, and a night that symbolized loneliness and rejection—regardless of the daylight shining all around him.

And, I thank God that the Bible records the *night* experiences of Jesus because it lets us know that Jesus conquered the night, to let us know that, we too can handle our dark night experiences.

If Jesus persevered, then so can you! If Jesus stood in the midst of his midnights, then so can you! If Jesus made it through his Gethsemane, if he could say *nevertheless* to the will of God for his life, then so can you! For we know that even though He suffered mighty, he did not let the night beat him! Tell someone near you: *Don't let the night beat you!*

For some of us, night is unemployment, while for others, it's getting up and going to a job we hate. Night for some is being sick, knowing that there is no cure for what ails you. Night is living in a loveless marriage. Night is raising rebellious children. Night is sacrificing for ungrateful family members who never have anything to give you but a request for more of what they need. Night is working day and night and still not being able to get ahead. Night is loving your neighbor even though they continue to spit in your face. Yes, every body has his or her night situations—our dark nights of the soul!

When Jesus hung on Calvary's cross—many thought that that was the end, that he was defeated. Many thought that Jesus had given up when he cried out—*My God, My God, why hast thou forsaken me?* When he cried out, *IT IS FINISHED*, many others thought he had really given up hope. But Jesus could not bear his father allowing them to be separated. Did not Jesus say, *I and the Father are one, if you have seen me, you have seen the*

Father. But it seemed that God had forsaken him and that God had turned his back on the Son of God.

But we must understand that the ALL HOLY GOD *had* to turn his back on Jesus as he hung on a cross at Calvary. He had to because at that moment, he who had never committed a sin, became sin. Jesus became the sacrificial lamb—offered up for your sins and for my sins. He took MY place on Calvary's cross. He bore the weight of the world's sins once and for all. In those hours, the one who had never committed murder, became a murderer. The one who had never lied, became a liar. The one who had never committed adultery, became an adulterer. The one who had never hated his neighbor, became jealous and envious of those around him.

Oh yes, Jesus felt the shame of every sinner, and bore the blame of every sinner while he hung, bled and died on Calvary's cross! And God, the all Holy One, could not look at him at that hour, so that he might look at us today, and see us dressed in the righteousness of Christ! He could not look at sin on the cross but he can look at me, a sinner, because all GOD will see is the *Blood of Jesus* covering my unworthiness. He could not fellowship with Jesus that Dark Friday in order that he could fellowship with us today. Because that day on Calvary's Cross—Jesus changed places with me and bore my wretched sins; he nailed them to the cross! And my unrighteousness is covered in his righteousness! Hallelujah to Jesus!!!

WHEN Jesus cried out—*My God, My God, I JUST WANT TO KNOW WHY*, everyone thought that he had given up; that the *night* had beaten him! But, thank God, that was not his last word. Because after that he spoke of victory, when he said: *IT IS FINISHED!* He shouted with a great shout: *It is Finished! Tetelesta* is the Greek word for a victory shout. It is the cry of a man who has completed his task; it is the cry of a man who has won the struggle. Finally, it is the cry of a man who has come out of the DARKNESS into the glory of the light and has won the crown!

And church, I know that the NIGHTS of our lives get dark. I know about loads getting too heavy to bear. I know about wetting a pillow with tears, about pacing the floor in the midnight hour trying to figure out just what to do. But I got today to encourage somebody. Your night season is not the time to cry out—MY GOD, MY GOD, WHY HAST THOU FORSAKEN ME? Instead, I am here to tell you that your night season is the time to hold on until you can shout—*TETELESTIA*! SHOUT VICTORY! Hold on until you can shout: *I can see clearly now that the dawn has come!*

For God's sake, **DON'T LET THE NIGHT BEAT YOU**! Remember that if Jesus had given up in Gethsemane's garden, God's plan for our Salvation would have been frustrated. Our salvation was hanging in the balance as Jesus prayed: *Father, if it be thy will, let this bitter cup pass from me, but never-the-less, not my will, but thy will be done.* In Gethsemane, Jesus learned to accept what he could not understand: to trust God when life made no sense. And that's exactly what you and I must learn. We need to remember who said: *For I know the plans I have for you, plans to prosper you and give you a future and a hope, not to harm you.* So people of God, I am here to tell you: DON'T LET THE NIGHT BEAT YOU!

Nelson Mandella *held on* for 27 years in a dark South African Prison. Our foreparents held on through 300 years of slavery, and Jesus held on for 6 hours one Friday afternoon! Keep on holding on until you see the light at the end of the tunnel. Keep up the fight until your dawn breaks, until the sun comes bursting through the clouds, and until you make it to the other side of midnight.

Night is like a veil over us, for we cannot see clearly when we are in the middle of our night season. The apostle Paul wrote—*Now we see through a glass darkly,* but Jesus' Calvary experience shows us that if we hold on, even when it feels like God has deserted us, we can make it through the night. We can be victorious over whatever darkness life covers us in! Jesus is our example that we don't have to let the night beat us. For the text in St. Luke says: *He is not here, but He is risen as He said.*

What will it take for *you* to believe? Jesus refused to let the night beat him: his night of *betrayal*, the night of *denial*, the night of *rejection*, the night of *humiliation* and *shame*, the night of *loneliness*, the night of *crucifixion*, the night of *death*, or the two nights spent in *hell*. Jesus refused to let the NIGHT beat him! By doing so he left us the message: *I made it through my Dark Nights, so that you would know that YOU CAN TOO!* You can make it through, too! Though you walk through the valley of the shadow of death, fear no evil, for He is with you.

Unemployed? Don't let it beat you! Homeless? Don't let it beat you! Lonely? Don't let it beat you! Addicted? Don't let it beat you. Lonely? Rejected? Friends turn their backs on you? Don't let the night beat you! No matter what NIGHT SEASON you're going through, HOLD ON! Life may have you nailed to a tree, right now, but it does not have to beat you.

I know I'm right! The Bible backs me up! They thought that beating Jesus within an inch of his last breath would get rid of him. They thought that nailing him to the cross would get rid of Him. They thought that burying him in a borrowed tomb and sealing the tomb would keep him. And surely, they thought death would keep him or that hell's fire would finish him off!

But never forget that the darkest hour is always just before dawn! The devil had gotten comfortable on that Saturday night. The enemies of Christ, the self-righteous Jews—the Temple rulers, Herod and Pilot—finally rested from their undying efforts to destroy Jesus. But early Sunday morning a small group of women got up extra early and made their way to the place they had seen Joseph lay the body of Jesus wrapped in white linen cloths in a tomb. They were all prepared to properly prepare the body of their beloved Jesus with spices for burial. But they all got a Sunday morning Surprise. The stone had been rolled away! The guards were sound asleep. And when the women went into the tomb, they found NOT the body of Jesus, but his linen cloths. WHAT HAPPENED? WHO STOLE HIS BODY? WHY?

WHY? Because he refused to let the night beat him. He got up from the grave, just like he said he would. Nobody stole the body, he arose, with a transformed body and is *alive* forever more! And because Jesus got up, I can get up from whatever has its foot on my neck. I can come back from whatever has me defeated. I can rise up from my pitfalls in life. And so can you!

Because Jesus BEAT THE NIGHT, you and I can make it through our midnight seasons. Death could not keep Jesus down, the grave could not keep Jesus down; even hell could not keep Him. So DON'T LET THE NIGHT BEAT YOU!

Remember—Jesus got up on the third day with all power in His hand.

DON'T LET THE NIGHT BEAT YOU
St. Luke 24:1-9

STUDY QUESTIONS

1. What scriptures do you say when you feel like giving up?

2. What feelings from past hurts have kept you from moving beyond your night experience? Shame? Guilt? Not forgiving others?

3. How did you get through your last night experience?

4. What did you learn about yourself after surviving one of your night experiences?

5. What prevented you from moving closer to God before, during, or after one of your night experiences?

CHAPTER II

HOW TO CONQUER YOUR JERICHO

Joshua 1:1-3

Now after the death of Moses the servant of the Lord it came to pass, that the Lord spake unto Joshua the son of Nun, Moses' minister, saying, 2 Moses my servant is dead; now therefore arise, go over this Jordan, thou, and all this people, unto the land which I do give to them, even to the children of Israel. 3 Every place that the sole of your foot shall tread upon that have I given unto you, as I said unto Moses.

The city of Jericho represented for the Israelites an impenetrable force. Jericho was their point of impossibility. Jericho was the one city they felt was impossible to conquer. Jericho was test of their true power. The walls of Jericho stood before God's people as an impenetrable force: too high to climb over, too wide to knock down, and too strong to break through. Not only that, but when and if they got through there were the mighty armies of Jericho to contend with. But when they got to the Jordon River, they knew after they crossed they would have to conquer Jericho before they could truly inherit the land promised by God to their forefathers—Abraham, Isaac and Jacob. And so there stood mighty Jericho—blocking every promise God had made to them.

What Jericho is blocking God's promises for your life? What Jericho is blocking your blessing? What Jericho is blocking my blessing? What Jericho is blocking the blessings the church stands in need of? And please don't get holy and sanctified on me and tell me that you're satisfied with Jesus. Please don't tell me, "I'm believing God for my blessing" or that "God is going to work everything out in my life."

How can that be when I already know that you're as miserable this year as you were last year? I know you haven't achieved all that God would have you to achieve. I know that you are still stuck in your wilderness places and that you are letting giants keep you from crossing your Jordan River and conquering your Jericho Walls! But the text tells us those walls may not be as impenetrable as the enemy wants us to believe they are. Joshua's victory gives us hope that we too can conquer our Jericho. We can learn from Joshua and see that with God all things are possible! *How To Conquer Your Jericho?* Look at Joshua to learn how.

Listen to the Lord

If we would conquer our Jericho, we must first learn to listen to the Lord. In Joshua 1:1-3 (*New International Version*), we learn that after the death of the Lord's servant, Moses, the Lord spoke to Joshua who was the son of Moses' assistant, Nun. He said, *Now then, you and all these people, get ready to cross the Jordan River into the land I am about to give to them—to the Israelites.*

And in the verses that followed in Joshua 1, we learn that God promised to give them what he had promised to give Moses.

> *I will give you every place where you set your foot, as I promised Moses (3). No one will be able to stand up against you all the days of your life. As I was with Moses, so I will be with you; I will never leave you nor forsake you (5). Be strong and courageous, because you will lead these people to inherit the land I swore to their forefathers to give them (6). Be strong and very courageous (7).*

Now understand that in order for God to have an impact on Joshua, Joshua had to *be still* and *listen* to what God was saying. Joshua had to put his own thoughts aside. He had to put his own agenda aside. Listening takes energy. Listening takes concentration. Listening takes an open mind and heart when it comes to the things of God. Remember that popular TV commercial in the 1980s that said: *When E. F. Hutton speaks—people listen.* Well, I'm here to say to the people of God that when God speaks, we need to listen.

We need to be still, stop for a while, quiet down, take some time out, and listen to what God has to say. I know that Joshua listened because of what happened after God spoke to Joshua.

Believe What The Lord Says
Not only must we listen if we are to CONQUER OUR JERICHO, we must also believe what the Lord says. God told Joshua that he would be victorious for the rest of his life and that he would inherit the promise given to Moses. But in order for God's promise to come to pass, Joshua had to also believe what God said. But as you probably know, *believing is easier said than done.* To believe—to trust—is to have faith in what you cannot see. No matter how preposterous, far fetched, or impossible it sounds. If we are to reap the benefits of God's promises, we must believe.

Chapter 6 in the book of Joshua says that Jericho was shut up because of the children of Israel—*No one went out and no one came in.* Verse 2 of that chapter tells us more of what the Lord said to Joshua: *See I have delivered Jericho into your hands, along with its king and its fighting men.*

Know this! Everything changes when the Lord speaks. All we have to do is believe God. God says the impenetrable walls of Jericho will crumble like sand on a beach. God says—I know that the army of Jericho is great and powerful. I know that the wall is high and wide and the gates are tightly shut. But listen Joshua, *I am going to give you Jericho!*

Can't you see that it doesn't matter what proceeds a word like *BUT?* If the Lord says the walls of Jericho will come down, then they are coming down. I don't care how high, how wide, or how strong the walls in your life are, they too can crumble. It doesn't matter how many generations a curse has been in effect. It does not matter how long you've been in your predicament! When God speaks, powerful walls crumble, mighty armies melt in fear. I don't care what your unbelieving friends or family members have been telling you! Why shouldn't we believe? The PROMISES of God are still *YES* and *AMEN*!

Yes, you can conquer your Jericho if you only BELIEVE. **IMPOSSIBLE THINGS ARE HAPPENING EVERYDAY!** Old thing have passed away; all things have become new. You only have to remember to say that familiar phrase—*I can do all things through Christ who strengthens me!*

Have you ever noticed that God's promises to Joshua were spoken in the past tense? *See I have delivered Jericho into your hands, along with its king and its fighting men.* The men had not even not set foot in Jericho when God said, *It's already done.* In the movie *Sleeping With the Enemy,* there is a line at the end of the movie that fascinates me. Julia Roberts, the abused wife in the movie, overtakes her husband who is trying to kill her. After wrestling the gun from him she calls the police and tells the officer: *I just shot an intruder.* Notice that even though she had *not* pulled the trigger yet, her husband knew he was a goner. She did not say I'm going to shoot him or I might have to shoot him. She said I *shot* him. And the tense in God's promise is like that. It was also past tense when God said: *I have given you Jericho.*

Well, somebody needs to remember that all the blessings are ours, if we believe what the Lord says. Keep telling yourself—*IT'S A PAST TENSE PROMISE*!

Obey Even When You Don't Understand

By now it should be clear that there are two ways to CONQUER YOUR JERICHO: *listen* and *believe.* And, there's a third way—*obey God's instructions.* In other words, *do it God's way*! But the problem for too many of us is that we do just the opposite: we do not obey the word of God. If you're not going to let the night beat you and if you want to be able to conquer your Jericho, then it is time out for our being *just* hearers of the Word. We must be *doers* of the Word. Now is the time to OBEY the Lord even when it doesn't make sense. Joshua and his army may have drawn up some fine workable plans for the battle at Jericho. But the Bible tells us that God gave Joshua His battle plans. It's God's way, *NOT* our way!

I know we think we know it all. We think we know how to handle our situations. God's ways seem so antiquated to many of us. God's ways can seem so silly. That's why so many people don't obey. That's why we create our own battle plans and then get trapped in them. Young men in Baltimore may ask: *Why should I wait to become sexually active?* Well, after a few cases of sexually transmitted diseases they may change their mind. Listen, young men, after a few babies when you are not equipped emotionally or financially to handle the situation, you may not think God's way is so backwards.

My sisters, after getting your heart ripped out time after time by someone who just wanted a warm body, someone who just stopped by for a brief *bootie call* on his way to the next stop, you may wish you had waited for the man God *was planning* to give you to marry. God's way is not so stupid after all, is it? You might as well go ahead and tell yourself that starting right now, *I'll going to do things God's way.*

God definitely had a plan for Jericho. He told Joshua to gather the Priests, select seven to carry the Ark of the Covenant, and lead the people who were each to carry a ram's horn. Then, he told Joshua to have them march around the walls of Jericho one time, for six days—in total silence. On the seventh day, they were told to march around the city of Jericho seven times; on the seventh time the priests were told to blow the horns. After the people gave a mighty shout, God told Joshua the walls of the city would collapse and the people could then charge straight into the city.

You know the rest of the story. The people obeyed! They marched around the city and sounded the horns. The people gave a mighty shout, and the rest is history: the walls crumbled like sand castles when the tide comes up on the beach.

After Obedience Comes Victory

Did you notice that the victory came after OBEDIENCE? As crazy as the plan sounded, as stupid and as impossible as it sounded, the people followed God's instructions as given to them by His chosen leader, Joshua. Joshua followed the Lord; the people followed Joshua. And sure enough, their OBEDIENCE wrought them the VICTORY. So the message in this chapter is clear, if you want to conquer your Jericho do three things: LEARN TO LISTEN, LEARN TO BELIEVE, and LEARN TO TRUST AND OBEY GOD. In other words, we must learn to take God at his word and to do things His way. Our victories will only come after *Obedience*!

That should be clear since the Bible tells us that God's ways are not our ways and that God's thoughts are not our thoughts. What God says may not always make a lot of sense. There may not be a lot of logic in what God tells us to do. But, we can learn from Joshua, the Priests, and the ordinary people of God. What we will learn is that God's way is the *BEST WAY*! When Joshua followed God's *illogical instructions* to the letter, the Walls of Jericho came tumbling *down, down, down*. If I don't know anything else, I know that God's way brings VICTORY!

I saw that in 1997 when my church was preparing to build a beautiful, new sanctuary. The Lord spoke to my heart and gave me instructions to *cut out all fundraisers*. *"What!"* I said to myself, *"cut out fundraisers in the middle of a building program?"*

It sounded crazy to me and to others when I shared God's instructions. But we were obedient. Amazingly, that year and every year that followed, for the next five years, our church was able to raise more money than ever before. We did it from tithes, general offerings, and sacrificial offerings. No fundraisers were held because I knew and the church knew that God's way brings victory. *Hallelujah to the Lamb of God*!

Some years ago, the Lord told me to sit down the best sounding choir in our church because there was too much mess or confusion going on. "What!" I again said to myself. "God, you can't mean it. Some people come here *just* to hear that choir. The Sunday that the choir sings is always our best attended Sunday." I didn't like it. But I obeyed. And you should see what God has done with our Music Department; it's second to none anywhere! God's way works. It's His way not our ways that bring the victory. God's thoughts are not our thoughts, but God's ways are always right! Oh yes, beloved, let me say it again: after OBEDIENCE comes the victory!

The walls of Jericho came tumbling down. They came down not by the armies of Israel pounding on the Wall, not by them dropping bombs on the Wall, and not by them ripping the bricks out of the wall. The walls came tumbling down because the people obeyed God and did things His way. The sound of the horn and the shouts of the people brought that mighty structure down. As the young people would say, *Now how cool is that?*

I'm reminded of the Prophet Zechariah who said, *Not by might, nor by power, but by my spirit says the Lord of Hosts*! Yes, because of the blind obedience of God's people, they totally destroyed the most fortified city in the Land. Jericho had to come down because OBEDIENCE brings victory!

If you want your Jericho Walls to come down, then practice Obedience! It's not about getting a promotion or a raise in salary. It's not about getting married or divorced. It's not about getting a degree, a new house, or a new car. It's simply about *obedience* to God's Word. ***Obedience brings the victory***! If you don't believe me, ask Mary, the Mother of Jesus. At the wedding at Cana the wine ran out in the middle of the reception. Jesus gave his disciples some *illogical* instructions when he said, *Bring me the water pots from outside the door*. Can you imagine? The disciples probably thought that Jesus must have bumped his head. They knew the pots were dirty and that feet had been cleansed in them. But Mary told them—*do what ever Jesus tells you to do*. And when they obeyed, they ended up with the best wine ever.

Namaan also knows what it means to be obedient. He was a mighty man of valour and a leper. When God told him to go dip in the Jordan River seven times, he probably thought to himself, *What*? *You're asking me to dip seven times in some muddy water? And why seven, why not three—why not five*? But Namaan obeyed. And when he did he was healed of his leprosy. You see, obedience not logic brings VICTORY!

Then there's the case of the ten lepers. They were told: *Go show yourselves to the priest*! You can almost hear them thinking out loud, *Show the priest what? We are still lepers*. But as they went—as they obeyed—they were *healed*! Now that's obedience! Obedience brought victory; it still brings victory! What, you might ask, is God telling me about my Jericho? Whatever Jericho you are experiencing, you can be sure obedience will bring victory.

This is true for your high walls, your seemingly unconquerable situations, incurable diseases, unsatisfied desires, unmet needs, constant poverty, unhealed hearts, addictions, life threatening habits, ungodly ways, secret sins, and/or unfulfilled relationships. Your JERICHO—your tall, your wide, your impenetrable Jericho walls will fall when you obey God.

Now is the time to submit your ways and wills to the One who causes walls to crumble. If you think that change is impossible in your life, it might help to remember that *impossible things are happening everyday*. What was the last miracle you experienced? Who did you share it with? The evidence that obedience to God works is already embedded in the scriptures and the lives of many. Have we not heard: *If God be for you, what is the whole world against you!* I know your walls seem impenetrable, but I also know that there is nothing God cannot conquer when we *trust and obey*. His word says: *Be ye transformed by the renewing of your minds*. Isn't it time to start repeating on a daily basis—*IT'S GOD WAY OR NO WAY*!

God's way is not only the *best* way, it is the *only* way to real and lasting VICTORIES!

God wants us to have VICTORIES!   That's why the Word of God assures us that we are more than conquerors! Doesn't it feel good to say this?

> *Victory is mine, Victory is mine,*
> *Victory is mine today.*
> *I told Satan, get thee behind me,*
> *Victory is mine today!*
> *Joy is mine.*
> *Peace is mine....*

Want to know how to conquer your Jericho walls?

Learn to *listen, believe*, and *obey!*

Practice saying everyday—*Obedience brings Victory!*

Obedience brings victory!

Then you'll know how to conquer *your* Jerichos!

HOW TO CONQUER YOUR JERICHO
Joshua 1:1-3

STUDY QUESTIONS

1. Describe the Jericho walls in your life.

2. When was the last time you were quiet and still in the presence of the Lord?

3. List some of the promises that God has made to you?

4. In what ways have some of God's promises come true for you?

5. Describe an experience when you did not understand where God was leading you, but you obeyed him anyway?

CHAPTER III

DESPERATE PEOPLE PRAY
DESPERATE PRAYERS

1 Samuel 1:9-11

So Hannah rose up after they had eaten in Shiloh, and after they had drunk. Now Eli the priest sat upon a seat by a post of the temple of the LORD. 10 And she was in bitterness of soul, and prayed unto the LORD, and wept sore. 11 And she vowed a vow, and said, O LORD of hosts, if thou wilt indeed look on the affliction of thine handmaid, and remember me, and not forget thine handmaid, but will give unto thine handmaid a man child, then I will give him unto the LORD all the days of his life, and there shall no razor come upon his head.

The Bible lets us know that although Hannah was a married woman, she was *not* a happily married woman. We all know that every marriage is not happy. Hannah's husband, Elkanah, loved her and gave her a double portion of offering time; but, still, Hannah was not happy. The source of her unhappiness was that she had no children. In addition to that, Peninnah, Elkanah's other wife, who had born several children for Elkanah, was a cruel, insensitive woman. The Bible says that Hannah's adversary, or her rival, provoked her till she wept and would not eat, because the Lord had shut up Hannah's womb.

Hannah's husband did not understand why she was unhappy; he even asked her in verse eight, *...am not I better to thee than ten sons?* Some women seem to think marriage will make you totally happy and fulfill all your dreams. As we read this portion of Scripture about this married woman, we are reminded that marriage will not solve all of our problems. As a matter of fact, if we're honest, marriage may add to our problems. Hannah was married, but Hannah's life was unfulfilled because she had no children, and she desperately wanted to give Elkanah children. Hannah was a desperate woman.

Why Hannah Was So Desperate?

Hannah was desperate because of her barrenness. As you might recall, Old Testament women were given honor by the number of children they produced for their husbands. If the children were male children, the women received more honor. If a woman produced no sons, the husband's entire inheritance would go to the other wives' sons, or even the slaves. Because of this, a barren woman was a woman of scorn; she was a woman with little self-esteem or joy. In Genesis 11:30, the biblical description of Sarai reads *but Sarai was barren*. Remember, whenever you see this word 'but,' it is a contravening conjunction. 'But' cancels out everything that came before it. Remember the story of Naaman in the fifth chapter of II Kings. The Bible said that Naaman was the captain of the host of Syrians, 'but' he was a leper. Sarai was beautiful, 'but' she was barren; she was married to a prosperous man, 'but' she was barren. She carried the stigma of being a "barren woman" everywhere she went.

Being barren, even though she had a husband who desperately loved her, made Hannah a *desperate* woman. She desperately wanted to give her husband a son.

Hannah was also desperate because Peninnah, her husband's other wife, teased her and taunted her; her rival made her feel even worse about the situation. It was just like Hagar who taunted Sarai when she found that *she* was having a child for Abram; she knew Sarai had not conceived. She taunted Sarai and teased her: *He comes to my tent more often than he comes to see you.* Hagar taunted Sarai. And, Peninnah taunted Hannah.

Hannah was desperate because of her barrenness, and because her rival, Peninnah, provoked her severely because the Lord had closed Hannah's womb. But I want to suggest that every Hannah needs a Peninnah. I firmly believe that we all need a little push every now and then, in order for us to be productive. I'll use myself as an example.

I've always been a stubborn person. The moment you tell me that I can't achieve something, that's when I'll try all the harder! My great-grandmother taught me that "they whipped ole *can't* till he said he *could*." I try to live by that attitude. I know that *I can do all things through Christ who strengthens me.*

Sometimes we need to be provoked, don't we? We have to get angry before we'll rise up. We need to be challenged before we'll rise up. Sometimes, in order to move from where we are to where we need to be, we need somebody to aggravate us just one time too many before we'll take action. I work harder than some as a pastor just because I'm a woman. I preach hard, pray hard and fight hard, because they said a woman couldn't make it as a pastor in the church. Often, it comes from being provoked. I tell you, every Hannah needs a Peninnah!

Desperation Will Move You To Desperate Actions

My sisters and brothers, if this story teaches us nothing else, it teaches that desperation will move you to desperate actions. Hannah was moved to desperate actions because of her barrenness and because Peninnah taunted her.

Every woman needs to know that this can work in more than one way. Our desperate actions can be positive or they can be negative. Some women have been known to do drastic things out of their desperation. Remember that desperation means a state of hopelessness leading to rashness, or to irrational behavior. Like Sarai, who gave Hagar to her husband to produce a child; like Tamar, who took off her widow's clothing and disguised herself as a prostitute in order to sleep with her father-in-law, Judah, because she was desperate to have a baby. Like Rachel, who traded the privilege of sleeping with Jacob, her husband, for Leah's mandrakes, a fertility potion—people do desperate things. If you and I are honest, we can write our own stories. Desperate people do desperate things!

Desperation will move you into taking some kind of action. Out of her desperation, the text said that Hannah cried, would not eat, and would not go to the temple. She probably nagged her husband over something that was not within his control. Have you ever done that? Have you ever blamed others for something over which they had little or no control. Some people commit suicide *out of desperation.* Some become addicted to drugs or alcohol. Some women lower their moral and Christian standards out of desperation to find a man. Then, they do anything to keep him, once they get him.

Desperation will move you to desperate actions. Some women suffer constant physical and verbal abuse from their husbands or lovers, because they are desperate to keep them. Some women knowingly share their mates with other women because of desperation. I've heard desperate women say, *Half of a loaf is better than none at all.b* That's a sure sign of desperation! Desperation will move you to some kind of action, either positive or negative.

Rise, Sally, Rise

In First Samuel 1:9 we read that *Hannah rose up after they had eaten in Shiloh and after they had drunk.* Some of you might remember some rhymes from our childhood days when children still played children's games. My family was poor, so we lived in the projects in Raleigh, North Carolina. When I was a little girl we did not have a lot of toys so we made up our own entertainment. Our mothers would sit on the porch in the early evening and watch us play children's games in front of the house. I'm reminded of those days whenever I read the line in the Bible that says, *so Hannah rose up...* It brings back memories of a game from my childhood. We would form a circle; one girl would get in the middle and act it out as we all sang:

> *"Little Sally Walker sitting in a saucer. Rise, Sally, rise; dry your weeping eyes. Put your hands on your hips and let your backbone slip. Shake it to the east; shake it to the west; shake it to the very one that you love the best."*

I liked the idea of little Sally Walker rising up. The text in First Samuel lets us know that Hannah rose up. I contend that Hannah rose up out of desperation. She was sick and tired of being *sick and tired*. She put her hands on her hips and did something about her situation. She rose up! She went to the Temple and prayed.

Now you know that we all know that life has a way of knocking us so far down that getting up sometimes doesn't even cross our minds. Yet, Hannah's story lets us know that we don't have to wallow in our mess; we don't have to drown in our tears. We, too, can **rise Sally rise**. We can put our hands on our hips, and keep on keeping on. You and I know that when a *sister* puts her hands on her hips, she means business, and you had better move out of her way! Are you desperate enough to pray with your hands on your hips?

Too Low Down To Pray

I have also found that sometimes a lot of folks are *too low down* in their desperation to *even* pray. Even though we know that prayer works and that prayer changes things, sometimes some of us can't even get a prayer through. But the key is *to rise up...* Just when it looks like the night is about to beat you and just when it looks like your Jericho wall is not going to fall, look at Hannah! The Bible says that first, *she rose up.* You must understand that sometimes you have to *get up,* before you can pray. You got to determine in your heart that no matter what the problem is, you are not going to let it keep you down and out. You've got to get up and take some action. We've got to do exactly as Hannah did—RISE UP! Remember? *So, Hannah rose up*!

But take another look at what Hannah *actually* did. She actually *rose up* so she could *bow down* before the Lord. Now isn't that something. Our desperation is often a state of mind! Hannah's mind was confused; her mind was in such anguish that she could not even get a prayer through. Yet, she had to take control of her mind before she could go before the Lord and ask for what she needed. First Samuel 1:10 says, *She was in bitterness of soul, and prayed unto the Lord and wept.*

I see a clue there for us, don't you? Rising up does not necessarily mean that all is well! Rising up does not necessarily mean that our problems are solved. It certainly didn't mean that Hannah solved her problem or that her situation had changed or that she no longer had problems. It definitely did not mean that Hannah was no longer hurting or no longer had tears in her eyes or that her heart was no longer broken. Her situation simply lets us know that *we've got to take some positive steps toward solving our own problems!*

Look at what happened. Hannah *had to* rise up *before* she could get down on her knees to ask for help. *So, Hannah rose up.* She decided to stop drowning in her own tears; she decided to stop nursing her pain. She was sick and tired of that same old solitary pity party. *So, Hannah rose up*! She rose up simply because she was desperate. If I know nothing else, I know that desperate people can rise up. I know that desperate people pray desperate prayers.

If you are a mother or father, and have not had to pray a desperate prayer, don't sit around criticizing other desperate people. Just because your marriage is working out—right now, that is—don't you dare criticize any other person's faltering marriage; your turn may be coming. Today's parents are forced to pray desperate prayers for their children. They may not be bad children, but there are bad people in our communities. We have to pray because there are drug dealers whose purpose is to sell drugs to young children, or hire young children to sell drugs for them. There are teachers who will sexually abuse your sons and daughters; there are pimps who want to turn your beautiful daughters into prostitutes. There are confused young men driving through neighborhoods randomly spraying bullets that cripple and kill young boys and girls who have done nothing more than dare to play in front of their homes.

Desperate parents *must* pray desperate prayers for their children. We are living in the first generation where children are killing children in mass. At the same time, our children are producing innumerable babies out of wedlock; babies who are often crack addicted babies, heroine addicted babies, HIV infected babies and unwanted babies. More than in any other generation, parents need to rise up and pray! Don't forget to pray for all our young people, not just your own children. As a well-known African proverb reminds us, *It takes an entire community to raise one child.* Desperate people must pray desperate prayers. We are in this thing together!

Hannah Rose Up And Prayed

So, Hannah rose up and went to the Temple—to the house of prayer. Notice, first of all, that she went alone. Prayer meetings are good, but you need to get into your secret closet every now and then and have a closed session with the Lord. Secondly, Hannah did not go to the priest and ask him to pray *for* her; she did not ask her husband to pray *for* her; Hannah prayed for her own self.

What did she pray? She did not pray that Peninnah would stop harassing her; she did not pray that Peninnah would be cursed. Rather, she prayed that God would open her womb. She prayed to God to give her a man child.

Hannah's Promise To God

In her prayer, Hannah promised God that she would give the child back to Him to become the Lord's servant. She promised God that she would raise the child as a Nazarite—a holy child—which meant that she was willing to invest some time into the raising of her child.

Herein lies an important clue for parents. As First Samuel 1:22 reveals...*But Hannah went not up; for she said unto her husband, I will not go up until the child be weaned, and then I will bring him, that he may appear before the LORD, and there abide for ever.* I believe that the problem with many of our children who are acting unseemly is that parents have not spent proper time raising them before leaving them with a television set and a key to the house to raise themselves. Our children need more lap time. They need to be loved everyday of their lives. I know that we have to work. I know what that's like; after all, I raised my son alone.

But sometimes we over react to this thing that we call "career enhancement." I know that our children have needs. I know what commercials, music and peer pressure are teaching our children. But I contend that they need our attention more than they need hundred-dollar sneakers and jeans. They need attention more than they need motorized bikes and athletic jackets. They need our attention more than they need store-bought hair and nails. They need constructive conversation more than hearing music that corrupts their young minds rather than corrects their misguided perceptions.

Hannah's story shows us that if more parents truly dedicated their children to the Lord, instead of just participating in a baptismal ceremony for show—for form and fashion—our children would be better off. Hannah shows us that if we bring our children to the temple for prayer; if we bring them to the temple for Sunday School or Bible study; if we bring them to the temple for worship, our children will grow up like Samuel and serve the Lord with a pure heart. I believe we would see a change in our children if we gave them more lap time.

Take Your Burdens To The Lord And Leave Them There

So, Hannah rose up! Hannah prayed a desperate prayer. She turned her problem over to the Lord; she released it to the one who had the power to do something about it. Hannah wanted the Lord to perform a miracle for her. She wanted to become a mother. She was so desperate that she could not even form the words. She prayed from her heart—her lips moved but no words came out. I don't know about you, but sometimes there are just no words to express what I need. The old folk of the church say that sometimes you just have to moan to the Lord.

After she prayed, she stopped worrying. Take a lesson from Hannah. If you worry, don't pray; if you pray, don't worry. Verse 18 says, after Eli had blessed her, had touched and agreed with her in prayer: *so the woman went her way, and did eat, and her countenance was no more sad.*

Sisters and brothers, desperate prayers get divine answers!

I know that's right!
Prayer changes things!
Prayer changes lives!
Hannah went from weeping to rejoicing!
In other words, Hannah rose up!
We all need to develop a Hannah mentality!
We need to learn how to rise up!

But I like the way my childhood rhyme describes it best.

Rise Sally, rise, dry your weeping eyes. Now put your hands on your hips and let your backbone slip. Shake it to the east; shake it to the west; shake it to the one that you love the best.

Hannah defied the odds and called her barrenness a lie. She knew that if God be for her, who in the world could be against her. She knew that God would give her the desires of her heart.

She knew that no weapon formed against her would prosper. Hannah rose above her limitations and used the only thing she knew that could change her situation—she prayed a desperate prayer!

Her verb and subject might not have agreed, but she prayed her prayer!

She might not have made much sense to Eli—he thought she was drunk, but she prayed her prayer!

Everyone else might have thought she was praying in vain, but Hannah prayed anyway!

So Hannah rose up!

Now it's time for you to rise up!

It's time for you to do what you've got to do after you've prayed those desperate prayers.

Rise, my sisters and brothers, RISE!

Rise! Rise! Rise!

DESPERATE PEOPLE PRAY
DESPERATE PRAYERS
1 Samuel 1:9-11

STUDY QUESTIONS

1. Looking back over your life, who has been your Peninnah? What feelings did you experience? What was your response?

2. Have you ever been so low you felt like you couldn't even pray? What did you do?

3. On a scale of 1-10, how would you rate your prayer life?

4. According to the message in the sermon, "desperate prayers get divine answers." In what ways have some of your desperate prayers been answered?

5. Using the text as an example, what two ways might you encourage a friend in a desperate situation?

DESPERATE PEOPLE PRAY
DESPERATE PRAYERS
1 Samuel 1:9-11

STUDY QUESTIONS

6. What prevented Hannah from being happy in her marriage?

7. When in the last six months did you recognize that you needed help from someone other than yourself?

8. What caused you to finally rise out of a desperate situation?

9. Who taught you how to pray?

CHAPTER IV

WHERE ARE YOU COMING FROM?
WHERE ARE YOU GOING?

Genesis 16:7-9

And the angel of the LORD found her by a fountain of water in the wilderness, by the fountain in the way to Shur. 8 And whither wilt thou go? And she said, I flee from the face of my mistress Sarai. 9 And the angel of the LORD said unto her, return to thy mistress, and submit thyself under her hands.

Do You Know Where You're Coming From?

A careful examination of this story of Abram, Sarai and Hagar will reveal in no uncertain terms, the pain that men and women suffer at the hands of other men and women. This story clearly shows that in relationships, it is not always men that ultimately cause women to suffer, or vice-versa, but women can, and do very often, cause other women to suffer just as men can, and do very often, cause other men to suffer. I contend that this story is about pain that two women inflicted upon each other, because they did not know where they were coming from and where they were going.

This story is not just about Sarai and Abram, but it is about women relating to other women. I have found that many of the problems in our churches and our homes stem from the fact that women cannot get along—cannot exist with other women. It saddens me to report that often, women can become enemies, instead of sisters. They can become separated over situations that evolve from our relationships with men, especially when more than one woman has an interest in the same man.

But, to the contrary, I want to suggest that a woman can find no better friend than another woman. I contend that a man cannot understand a woman like another woman can, simply because women have so many things that are peculiar only to women. There are experiences that women have that men find very difficult to relate to or to understand, simply because these experiences are "*for women only*."

Although a man is a part of the conception of a baby, the delivery of that baby is something he cannot speak to experientially. In other words, he may be the best gynecologist in town, but he has never had the experience of delivering a baby. He can be in the delivery room; he can be the coach who tells the woman to "push" or he can take videos. But until he's had a baby, he will never know exactly how it feels.

Women need other women in their lives. A woman who has undergone a mastectomy or hysterectomy is able to bring more comfort to another woman than a man who doesn't even have the anatomy for such an operation. We need each other because there are some experiences that are "for women only" and men just don't understand. It's not that they may not want to understand or to be compassionate, but they just don't have the capacity to walk a mile in a woman's shoes.

Although a woman never can (and was not designed to do so) take the place of a man in a woman's life, I contend that *every sister needs a sister*.

Differences And Similarities
We have a women's mentoring group at the church where I pastor in Towson, Maryland; we call it **Sisters Sharing**. We have spent about three years studying certain pericopes or passages of Scripture from a female hermeneutic—that is from a feminist or womanist interpretation. During our studies the Lord revealed some new insights about the lives of women in the

Bible. In one of our sessions we focused on Sarai, Abram's wife and the Egyptian slave girl, Hagar. When you begin to study the Word of God from a female perspective, you end up being able to put some flesh on the women in the Bible. So it is today as we examine the lives of Sarai and Hagar, we will see that women who are out of relationship with each other are often out of the will of God.

First, we learn that although Sarai and Hagar had many opposites, they also had much in common. Sarai was a beautiful, rich, Jewish woman, married to the highly esteemed Abram who loved her and wanted her to be happy. She had at her fingertips any material thing she desired. She had a husband who loved her; she had wealth; she had maids, such as Hagar. Sarai had everything, but she let one thing, her barrenness, ruin her life.

Hagar was a poor African slave girl who later became Abram's wife not because Abram loved her or because she loved Abram, but because her mistress, Sarai, gave Hagar to Abram for the sole purpose of bearing a son. Sarai's hope was that the son God had promised would come from the seed of Abram.

Not only were they different in their races—one a Jew and one African—they were also different economically. One was a rich slave owner and the other, a poor slave girl. But Sarai was old and barren and Hagar was young and fertile. Even with these vast differences, we begin to see the similarities between these two women—one Jewish, one African, one rich and married, one poor and a slave and one old and barren while the other was young and fertile.

Although there were many opposites, they still had similarities. Remember sister, the mere fact that you are woman means that you automatically have some things in common. They both lacked self worth. About Sarai, the Bible tells us in Genesis 16:1: *Now Sarai Abram's wife bare him no children: and she had an handmaid, an Egyptian, whose name was Hagar.*

Dr. Renita Weems[1], in her book entitled, *Just A Sister Away* says Sarai's honor rises and falls in that one line.

In ancient times, a woman's self-worth and social status pivoted around her family—the number of children she had birthed, preferably male children. But Sarai was barren in a culture in which a woman's womb was her destiny (some of our young women seem to still fell that way). Sarai was a woman scorned. Thus, in spite of all she had, Sarai's self-worth was at an all time low.

But so was Hagar's, the Egyptian maid. For how can a woman feel good about herself when she is always at the beck and call of another woman? How can a woman feel good about herself when her every waking hour is consumed with taking care of the needs of another woman—a woman who because of her own low self-esteem is probably not always kind. You do know that "misery loves company" don't you? Sarai and Hagar both lacked self-worth.

Their Lack of Self-Worth Led to a Lack of Self-Definition

One of the great poets of our nation once wrote *to thine own self be true*. It is important that we know who we are, even if no one else really knows who we are! All too often we allow others to define who we are and what we are, and even what we can become. And believe you me, that's dangerous. After all, no one knows you like you know yourself. Sure, others can see things in you that you may not be able to see, or to help you recognize some hidden qualities about yourself. But no one should know you as well as you know yourself, except God, and God knows you better than you know yourself!

Sarai depended on her culture to define who she was. They called her barren because she could not give her husband children—heirs to his inheritance. They called her barren

---

1.   Renita Weems, *Just A Sister Away* (San Diego, California: Laura Media, 1988), p.2.

because there were no little "pitter-patter" of feet running around Abraham's mansion. The society she lived in called her barren (as if all a woman was good for was being barefoot and pregnant). Because she had no self-definition, she accepted society's definition of who she was; for Sarai was a marked and miserable woman. And remember that I said "misery loves company!"

Sarai's lack of self-definition caused her to make one of the greatest mistakes of her life. In Genesis 16:2, Sarai seems to suggest, *...perhaps I will be esteemed through her.* Sarai gave her maid, Hagar, to be her husband Abram's wife—that he might have children with her; the children would thus belong to Sarai because Hagar belonged to Sarai. And Sarai, because she lacked self-worth and self-definition, said *...perhaps I will be esteemed through her.* A lot of women are like that today; they push their children to become somebody great so they can get some of the glory. Or they marry a man who is popular or highly noted, thinking that this is going to automatically make them somebody.

In this case, Sarai tried to be esteemed through Hagar. My sisters, it's dangerous to try and find your identity through the pain or the loss of another woman. Anytime you or I have to make someone else miserable to get what we "think" we want, we will never, like Sarai, have any self-esteem. She wasn't even happy after Hagar got pregnant. In fact, she became irrational. Verse three says, *Sarai said to Abram: you are responsible for the wrong I am suffering. I put my maid in your arms and now she knows she is pregnant, she despises me.* She became beside herself and irrational!

Not only did Sarai lack self-definition, but Hagar could not define who she really was, either. Hagar could not see her own self outside of her service to Sarai. Look at what happens in the story—when Sarai gives Hagar to Abram and Hagar becomes pregnant—which is what Sarai "thought" she wanted, both women ended up miserable, confused, and irrational! As Genesis 16:4 notes: *But when Hagar saw that she had conceived, her mistress' honor was lowered in her eyes.* The *New International*

Version of the Bible reads, *When (Hagar) saw that she was pregnant, she began to despise her mistress.*

Do you see what's happening? Because Hagar lacked self-definition, she now wants to take Sarai's place. Hagar now feels that she is more important to Abram than Sarai. Hagar now tries to make herself feel important by making Sarai feel small and insignificant because of her bareness. Can't you hear her? *I can have his baby and you can't. He desires me, not you. I'm what he needs; I can give him children. What can you do for him?* The Bible says Hagar taunted Sarai!

This is the only way Hagar can feel important—by putting another woman down. The same principal applies to Hagar that applied to Sarai. It's dangerous to try and find your identity or satisfaction through the pain and loss of another woman by hurting other women to get what you think you want! Remember, if you could easily take him, someone can take him from you.

They both lacked self-worth and they both lacked self-definition. As a result, not only was Abram and Sarai's marriage almost ruined, but God's plan for Abram and Sarai to be the father of many nations was put in jeopardy! Also, God's plan for Hagar and Ishmael was threatened.

Not Only Did They Lack Self-Worth And Self-Definition, They Also Lacked Self-Direction

Neither woman knew what she wanted. Sarai thought she wanted Hagar to have a baby that would ultimately be her baby. (We call it surrogate motherhood.) Hagar conceived, and then Sarai got jealous and angry with Hagar for following an order that she had given to her. Hagar didn't know what she wanted; so she ran away into the desert to escape the wrath of Sarai, a woman scorned. Two totally different women end up having the same problems. Neither one knew the direction that she should have taken to have had things turn out differently.

My sisters, this ought to teach us something—never judge a book by its cover. She may look like she has it all together; she may look like the happiest woman in the church; and she may seem to have everything you've always wanted. Her husband may seem to be perfect, and her children obedient, but you have not been behind closed doors with her; you haven't seen the tracks of her tears and you haven't felt her pain. Don't ever wish you were somebody else until you walk a mile in his or her shoes!

Every Sister Needs A Sister

We discovered in our *Sisters Sharing* groups at Mount Calvary A.M.E. Church, that women who have problems getting along with other women usually have problems with themselves. How can you say that you can't get along with women; aren't you a woman? Sarai needed a sister-friend to talk her through the situation and help her rationalize the situation when she had become irrational. A sister-friend might have said, "Now wait a minute, Sarai, you don't really want to send your husband in to that fine young thing's tent, do you? Girl, you had better think and pray hard and long before you make a move as serious as that, girlfriend!"

The saddest part about the entire story of Sarai and Hagar is that they could have been friends rather than enemies. I know about their differences; but understand this, my sisters, even with all of their differences, they still had enough in common that they could have become friends rather than foes. They could have supported one another; they could have worked together; they could have become a blessing to one another.

My sisters, don't ever think that another woman can't be a blessing to you because you live in the penthouse and she lives in the public housing projects; because you attended college and she didn't finish middle school; because you are married and she is single with three babies; because you are black and she is white; because you shop in fancy malls and she shops at the Goodwill.

You don't know what wisdom she has in her bosom. She may be ragged, old and gray, but I'll bet she's got more common sense than most of us. You might find, if you were to permit it, that she could be the best friend you've ever had. *Every sister needs a sister*!

Where Are You Coming From?
Where Are You Going?

Neither of these women had much self-worth, self-definition, or self-direction. And if the truth is told, not many of us clearly know where we are coming from and where we are going. Life is not always that simple. It would be wonderful to always be on top of our own lives, but that's certainly not always the case. Not with me, anyway!

But I thank God that when we don't know which way to go, God will intervene and show us the right way. Know that when you're hurting so badly that you want to hide from everybody, even God, He always knows just where to find you.

This was the case in Genesis 16:7 when we hear about Hagar. *And the angel of the LORD found her (Hagar) by a fountain of water in the wilderness ...* Later in Genesis 16:13 we are told, *And she called the name of the LORD that spake unto her, Thou God seest me: for she said, Have I also here looked after him that seeth me?*

This is one of the most powerful statements in the Bible for me, because every woman longs to be understood for just who she is. The angel knew exactly who Hagar was. Hagar needed an identity of her own. My sisters, if we cannot find our true identity in God, where can we find it?

That's a powerful statement. You may lack self-worth and you may lack self-definition. It may seem that your life has no direction right now. But know that there is a God who sees you and knows who you are. More importantly, God knows where you are coming from and where He can take you. All you need to do is what Hagar finally did—see the One who sees you.

He'll give you a higher level of self-esteem; he'll give you a positive self-definition.

God will tell you who you are in His eyes and He'll lead you in the right direction. God knows where you're coming from and He knows where you can go if you just keep your hand in His hand. When you are not clear about where you are going, God knows.

God sees you. Now you must see God!
He's your burden bearer!
He's your bridge over troubled waters!
He's your water in dry places!
He's your help when you're helpless!
He's the God who sees and loves you, and wants you to
    see Him so you can love yourself and love
    your sisters!
He will set you free to love!
He'll lead you and carry you through.

As the song says: *What a wonderful change in my life has been wrought, since Jesus came into my life...*

With Jesus you don't have to wonder where you are going or where you are coming from because he already knows the answer.
Amen?
Amen!
Amen!

WHERE ARE YOU COMING FROM?
WHERE ARE YOU GOING?
Genesis 16:7-9

STUDY QUESTIONS

1. Name three women who have been a blessing to you in your life?

2. Can you recall a time a time when you hurt someone because you were jealous? Did your response show that you were moving towards or away from God?

3. How did you learn self-worth? To what extent is your self-worth based upon the Word of God? Read Psalm 139:14 for biblical support.

4. What would prevent you from mentoring a man or woman from a different background?

5. When was the last time you asked God to reveal His plans for your life?

CHAPTER V

DRIED UP BROOKS

1 Kings 17:12
And she said, As the LORD thy God liveth, I have not a cake, but an handful of meal in a barrel, and a little oil in a cruse: and, behold, I am gathering two sticks, that I may go in and dress it for me and my son, that we may eat it, and die.

Chapter seventeen of First Kings shows God working with and through the life of the great prophet, Elijah. In this chapter, Elijah incurred the wrath of King Ahab and his wicked wife, Jezebel, after he prophesied that there will be no rain in the land these many years. After being threatened by Ahab and his wicked wife Jezebel, Elijah obeyed God and went to rest by the Brook Cherith where the ravens were commanded to feed him. The brook provided water until after a time when, the Bible says, *the brook dried up.*

Elijah further obeyed God and moved from isolation to involvement whereby he went to Zarephath where a widow was commanded to provide for him until the Lord gave him further instructions. We can learn from the prophet Elijah the art of trusting God, and obeying God, no matter how difficult the situation. For some of us, that is not always easy to do. But God promises support by the most unlikely candidates—a raven and a widow woman. Somebody needs to learn that blessings don't always come from where we expect them.

As we focus on the theme **Dried Up Brooks**, we find Elijah entering Zarephath where he encounters a widow woman gathering sticks for a fire. I want to focus our attention on this widow woman whom the Bible does not even dignify by giving her a name—she is only known by the region in which she lives. This may actually be best, because we'll find that in many instances, we can insert our name in the text.

Brooks Will Dry Up

This episode in the life of this great prophet shows us that his Brook Cherith—his supply, his substance, his lifeline—dried up on him. I want to remind us all that life is like that sometimes, and even our brooks will dry up on us every now and then. I don't care how saved, sanctified and filled with the Holy Ghost you are, your brooks will dry up on you every now and then.

That good government job, that large bank account, your social security check, your retirement bonus—let your welfare payments run out and watch your brook dry up. If your 25-year marriage ends up in divorce court—that's a dried up brook! If your entire family is killed in a senseless bombing—that's a dried up brook! The doctor reports that your loved one's sickness is unto death—that's a dried up brook. You're ready and prepared to go to college; even got accepted by the school of your choice, and your loan is denied—that's a dried up brook. Your son, or your wife, or your husband, or your daughter is hooked on drugs—that's a dried up brook. You're diagnosed HIV positive—that, my friend, is what I call a *dried up brook*!

I want to submit to you that this woman's brook, this widow of Zarephath, had dried up on her too many times. First of all, understand that she was born a female during a time when it was not popular to be a woman. In fact, it's not all that popular today, either. But in biblical times, fathers prayed for sons, not daughters. Men rejoiced when sons were born and cried over daughters.

A woman owned no property; a woman had no viable employment; a woman didn't even have full say so over her own life. She was always under a man's rule—first, father and then a husband. She was always serving others; always at another's beck and call; always trying to please—in the kitchen and in the bedroom, rather than being pleased by someone. This widow was a female during a time when a woman's main occupation or purpose was making and raising babies. If you didn't have children for your husband, you were a woman scorned (like Sarai, Hannah and Rachel).

Well, she was a widow and that signified she had at least once been a wife. She had belonged in someone's life. She had a place in society because of her husband. But, now, that that brook had dried up. Now, she was alone; now, she was a widow. She didn't even have the good fortune to have married a man with brothers. She was a widow. She knew about brooks drying up. Ever felt abandoned?

This widow had been a mother, but that brook dried up, too. A part of the joy of motherhood is having a husband to help you raise your children, to share the victories and the defeats of parenthood, and to share the expenses of parenthood—both mental and physical. Raising children properly is no easy thing! That's why I can't understand why my young sisters keep getting tricked into having a baby when their guy hasn't even given them a commitment—neither his name nor his paycheck! One thing about this woman, at least, she could be called a widow.

Hey young ladies, you can be *his* woman or *his* common-law wife. You can be the mother of his children, but if the brother doesn't marry you, you can't even be his respected widow! When this widow's brook dried up, she had to raise her son alone. I tell you, this widow woman was all too familiar with brooks drying up on her. I don't care what anybody says, if enough brooks dry up on you, you could end up in the same pitiful place that this woman was now in—gathering sticks and getting ready to eat her last meal and die!

She had a legacy of dried up brooks. Let me tell you, my sisters, let me tell you, my brothers, life is like that for a lot of us. That's why I said that we could insert our name in the text—any of us. It may not be a husband or a son that has become your *dried up brook*, but your brook of hope could dry up on you. It may be the brook of peace, the brook of joy, the brook of love, the brook of laughter or the brook of self-esteem. It may be the brook of beauty and desirability, the brook of a size "nine or ten dress," the brook of health, or the brook of wealth. Brooks *will* dry up on you.

Never Be Envious Of What Another Sister Has

A couple of years ago, Baltimoreans followed the story of our former city comptroller who was convicted of extortion. I listened with tears in my eyes as this beautiful fallen Black woman shared the story of her pain, her mental illness, her alcoholism (gin and vodka bottles were in her desk drawer), and her attempted suicide. Later in my bedroom, I said aloud to myself, *my God, her brooks have dried up on her!*

Most of us criticized the former City of Baltimore employee; some even condemned her. But let me warn you, right now! Never look down on another person who is in pain. Never kick people when they are down. You don't know what they are going through. You don't know what they have had to endure. Not only that, you need to be careful about wishing you had what another woman has—her job, her career, her husband, her home, or her position in life.

You have no idea what goes on behind her closed doors. You haven't walked a mile in her shoes. You haven't seen her tears. You don't know what brooks have dried up on her!

The widow woman's story and the story of Baltimore's comptroller, reflect a reality that suggests a life with too many dried up brooks can feel like a life not worth living. It can feel like you and I are gathering a few sticks ourselves and making our last meal—preparing to die. I believe the drying up of the widow's brook deserves more attention. Not only did her spiritual brooks dry up, but to top it all off, her physical brook also dried up. Even her water and food supply dried up. Now where would you turn when everything around you has dried up?

The Theology of "Somehow"

Let me assure you that it's hard to make it when brooks dry up on you and you *know* the Lord! Yet, you need to have a relationship with the Lord under all conditions. I surmised from reading 1 Kings 17:12 that the widow woman did not know the one true and living God for herself. For she says to Elijah in verse twelve, *as sure as the Lord your God lives...* She did not say *my God* or *our God.* She said *your God* and that signifies that God was not a part of her life.

The other reason I believe she did not know God in a personal way is that she had given up *all* hope. All hope! She had lost hope that a new brook would be opened to her. She said, *I'm gathering a few sticks to take home and make a meal for myself and my son, that we may eat it and die.* It's really is a terrible thing for your brooks to dry up and you don't know the one true and living God! Any true believer would know that the widow's statement was not the language of a believer. For when believers have nothing else to fall back on, they have hope!

Have any brooks ever dried up on you lately? I know first hand about dried up brooks. I grew up poor in the South. There were times when we didn't have much of anything; our needs were rarely met. Living in the projects of Raleigh, North Carolina where all the buildings looked alike, I wore hand-me-down clothes and hand-made skirts and blouses until I was able to work for myself. My mother was on welfare. My father was an alcoholic. My grandmother and my great-grandmother had no more than a third or fourth grade education. Yes, I had dried up brooks; I had some dark nights. Yes, I've seen some dreary days, and, I too have asked the Lord, "How long?"

But no matter how dark the night, no matter how desperate I was, and no matter how dreary the days became, I never gave up on God. I never gave up, no matter how hungry I was, no matter how many brooks dried up. You see, my uneducated great-grandmother taught me her homespun theology of "*somehow*." She said, *Child, the Lord will make a way, somehow*. I didn't know how, I didn't know when, but I grew up believing in "somehow. Somehow, there would be food on the table; somehow, we would keep a roof over our heads. Somehow... don't know how, but somehow.

I raised my son alone, *somehow*. And, after being out of high school for nine long years, God opened a door for me to attend Boston University. I was older than most Freshmen, but somehow I made it. I made the dean's list, became able to keep my young son while I lived on campus, and graduated with those who had been convinced that I wouldn't make it. After working at Harvard University and getting my first degree from Boston University, I wanted even more education. So I went on to get a Master's degree in theology and a Doctorate degree in ministry. I did it—somehow, somehow, somehow! When I felt like giving up, I could hear my grandmother saying, *Child, you can't hurry God, you just have to wait. He may not come when you want Him, but He's right on time*. Somehow!"

Maybe this widow woman once had faith and lost it. I don't know, but I know that she didn't know about the theology of *somehow*. She didn't know that the prophet Elijah's God was her *somehow*! She had given up all hope of surviving and had thrown in the towel. She didn't even have hope for her son. Some mothers and fathers, also seem today to have lost hope for their sons and daughters. For the widow woman, too many brooks had dried up and she wasn't planning on hanging around for the next episode. She needed a grandmother to tell her, *Your brooks may dry up, but the Lord will make a way, somehow!*

Now, when we first encountered this woman, she apparently felt as if she had nothing to lose! But what she didn't know was that she had everything to gain by obeying Elijah. The Bible says that she followed Elijah's instructions. She took care of the man of God first and, like clockwork, every time she went back for more Crisco oil, there was enough for the next meal. Do you know anything about hoecake bread? That's flour and water with a little oil fried on top of the stove. If you're too rich to know about hoecake bread, perhaps you've heard of "strick-a-lean" and "trick-a-fat." That was poor folk's bacon—more fat than lean meat. That's what they ate, day after day, after day; year, after year, after year until about three years later, when Elijah left.

A New Testimony

But don't think for a minute that all this woman got was flour and oil—that was the least of her blessings. Food and drink were not all this woman gained. Read 1 Kings 17:24 and listen to a new testimony from the widow woman.

> *And the woman said to Elijah, Now by*
> *this I know that thou art a man of God,*
> *and that the word of the LORD in thy*
> *mouth is truth.*

Giving her flour and oil every day did not necessarily develop that kind of faith in this woman. Giving handouts to the community will not necessarily develop its faith—people will end up just knowing where to come when times get hard.

Look at 1 King 17:18—after the widow's son got sick and died.

> *And she said unto Elijah, What have I*
> *to do with thee, O thou man of God? Art*
> *thou come unto me to call my sin to*
> *remembrance, and to slay my son?"*

As the Bible tells us, Elijah revived her dead son. Not long after, the widow found true faith. She could see that His power went beyond giving out bread and water; He restored life! That's a good reason right there to introduce every dying person we know to Jesus; only Jesus can give life. Only Jesus can restore life! Only Jesus can preserve life! The widow woman's son gained life through Elijah's prayer, and she gained faith through the life of her child. What a blessing! What Amazing Grace! Not only was her life extended, her *faith* was renewed, as well.

The widow no longer had just bread and water; she had a new testimony! She could say, *Now I know*! She wasn't going on Elijah's faith anymore. Now she could teach her own son *the theology of somehow*. She could say, *Son, when your brooks dry up on you, don't ever give up; the Lord will make a way, somehow.* Would you be able to say that or testify to others; would you be able to tell your children about *somehow* faith?

I don't know about you, but I'm glad I know the Lord for myself! And I shouldn't be alone in times like these.

We all need a personal relationship with God!

We need personal testimonies.

We need to know Jesus on a personal basis!

Yes, your brooks will dry up. For that is the nature of brooks! They are not designed to last always!

But brooks come from a greater source; Jesus is our river of living water!

Jesus is that fountain that never runs dry!

He's water when you're thirsty and bread when you're hungry!

Remember how He told the woman at the well that if she would drink from His well, she would never thirst again? Listen!

Somebody's brook has dried up. You know who you are!

You need to cry unto the Lord, *Fill my cup, Lord, I lift it up, Lord, come and fill the thirsting of my soul. Bread of heaven, feed me till I want no more. Fill my cup; fill it up and make me whole.*

One day I was that woman!

All my brooks had dried up.

The sad part about it was that I didn't even realize how thirsty I was. But one day, the Lord opened my understanding, and now "I know" that I had nothing to lose but everything to gain!

Just like Elijah came into the widow woman's life, Jesus came into my life!

He refilled my brooks!

He even led me to greater brooks!

He gave me new life!

Now I know that no matter how many brooks dry up in my life, the Lord will make a way, *somehow*. Jesus can do the same for you. Dried up Brooks? Jesus can make them flow again. Are you ready? Are you willing to say YES to Jesus?

DRIED UP BROOKS
1 Kings 17:12

STUDY QUESTIONS

1. Describe three brooks in your life that have dried up.

2. To what extent have dried up brooks affected your relationship with God?

3. In this message the widow did not know God in a personal way and as a result she felt hopeless. If people are Christians and have a personal relationship with God, is it possible for them to give up hope if it seems like there is no solution for their problems?

4. If someone you know is experiencing "dried up brooks" what advice or words of encouragement would you offer them?

5. What are the similarities and differences between the widow of Zarephath and the woman at the well?

CHAPTER VI

THE MIRIAM SYNDROME

Numbers 12:1;15-16

And Miriam and Aaron spake against Moses because of the Ethiopian (Cushite) woman whom he had married: For he had married an Ethiopian woman. 15 And Miriam was shut out from the camp seven days: and the people journeyed not till Miriam was brought in again. 16 And afterward the people removed from Hazeroth, and Pitched in the wilderness of Paran.

In this message we are going to look closely at the life of an Old Testament woman called Miriam—a very important character in biblical history. We first meet her in the book of Exodus where she is the first biblical woman to be called a *prophetess.* Not only is she a prophetess, but she is also a woman of praise. She is also the first woman to be seen in a leadership position because she led the women in praise after crossing the Red Sea.

Among many other things, the story of Miriam is important because it demonstrates that women are not simply footnotes in biblical history. Her story can teach all of us—both men and women—many things that will help us on our journey toward glory land.

Miriam's Life Shows That God Will Use Anyone

It becomes obvious to us from the very beginning that Miriam, the sister of Moses and Aaron, was on the Lord's side. It was obvious that Miriam was a leader after she stepped out front and lead the women in praise. It became clear that Miriam was a woman who feared God; a woman who loved God; a woman who followed godly instructions; and a woman who loved to praise God.

We have evidence in the Scripture that Miriam was on the Lord's side. Miriam knew that the Pharaoh was attempting to destroy all the newborn male Hebrews. So, Miriam assisted her mother, Jochabed, in the plan of God to preserve this future leader of Israel by hiding baby Moses in the Nile River and finding a nurse, his own mother, for him after the Pharaoh's daughter adopted baby Moses.

We must understand that the Lord will use us if we want to be used; if we have a sincere desire to be used; and if we make ourselves available for service. The problem in the church today is that every man and woman does not want to be used of the Lord. Oh, yes, we want to be a member of the church, we want to sing in the choir, usher at the door, serve as the Women's Day or Men's Day chair, head-up the women's ministries, but we do not necessarily want to submit and surrender to the will of the Lord Jesus Christ. We want to do it the way we want; we want to do what we want and we want to do it when we want. We do not really want to be used of the Lord.

If God's plans do not fit our plans, then, all too often God can forget it, because we just won't serve! We who are serious soon come to understand that being on the Lord's side is not as glamorous as many folk think it is. Miriam actually risked her life by showing up and offering a nurse for her baby brother. What if she had been questioned about her part in keeping this baby alive when the Pharaoh had ordered all males to be killed at birth? What if the Pharaoh had found out that Jochabed was really Moses' mother?

Being on the Lord's side can be a dangerous job. But many of today's Christians seem to want only the glamorous jobs. I received a phone call from a young woman who had heard a tape of a service I had preached in another state at a woman's conference. She went on to tell me that she wanted to know about my life as a minister and how I became a pastor and got the opportunity to speak all over the country. She said that she was asking because she was a public speaker and had thought about becoming a preacher. Well, to make a long story short, I told her that she could read my book, *...And Your Daughters Shall Preach*[1] to get a detailed description of my *call* into the ministry.

Two things struck me about that phone call. First, she never said that the Lord had called her to preach. Secondly, I wondered if she thought that getting where I am today had been an easy thing. That call and other comments have led me to believe that all too many women and men want the glamour of the position, but they are not willing to make the sacrifices necessary to get to a place where God can trust them to carry His Word and serve His people in a pastoral position.

My son, Lawrence, and I were talking one day about the lean days of my own ministry. He wanted to know how I could keep going for two-and-a-half years while preaching to a hand full of people, and living on a $100.00 a week salary. We lived in a dilapidated trailer home that was too hot in the summer and too cold in the winter. Lawrence asked me how I did it. I told him the Lord had called me to ministry, and to full-time service, and I had come to understand that if I could not "walk with footmen, I could never contend with horses."

It is mighty nice to be on the Lord's side, but it is also mighty hard sometimes to endure the hardship that it takes to serve the Lord.

Miriam and Jochabed were women on the Lord's side. They risked their lives to save one who would become Israel's greatest leader and lawgiver. They were rewarded by God because of their faithfulness, because they made themselves available to the service of the Lord.

---

1 Ann F. Lightner-Fuller, *...And Your Daughters Shall Preach: Developing a Female Mentoring Program in the African American Church.* (Towson, MD: *Little Sally Walker Ministries*, 2003)

My sisters and my brothers, God will use you if you want to be used; if you make yourselves available to the Lord.

Miriam, A Woman of Praise

> *And Miriam the prophetess, the sister of Aaron, took a timbrel in her hand; and all the women went out after her with timbrels and with dances. 21 And Miriam answered them, Sing ye to the LORD, for he hath triumphed gloriously; the horse and his rider hath he thrown into the sea.*   —Exodus 15:20-21

Miriam was an important leader in the priestly family which also consisted of Moses and Aaron and Miriam. Miriam was a prophetess called of God. She holds the singular distinction of being the very first female prophetess named in the Bible. That lets us know that God spoke to Miriam just as God spoke to Moses and Aaron. And so, Miriam surfaces as the leader of the women who led them well. We must understand that in the church today, too many women lead other women into contention, strife, division and backbiting. We bring our worldly ways into the church, and rather than glorifying God, we try to get glory for ourselves.

Pastors have to be very careful who is placed in leadership positions, because everyone cannot lead in a positive manner; everyone cannot work with other people—even in the church. Miriam surfaces as God's leader for the women of Israel after being delivered from Egypt. She obviously did a good job. For anytime we are lead to praise the Lord, that's a good thing. Anytime we are lead into greater service of the Lord, that's a good thing. The Bible says that she lead them joyfully with timbrels, and she lead them in dancing before the Lord. She taught them the appropriate response to God's goodness—that praise is appropriate—that the Lord inhabits the praises of his people.

She lead them in rejoicing; she showed them how to
praise the Lord for bringing them out of bondage into the
marvelous light. She taught them, like King David, to *make a
joyful noise unto the Lord, serve the Lord with gladness, come
into his presence with thanksgiving, and into his courts with
praise, for the Lord is good, and his mercy endureth for ever.*

The people of God must be taught that praise is comely,
and that the Lord loves to be praised. It is a good thing to give
praise unto the Lord. That is why I say, *I will bless the Lord at
all times, God's praises shall continually be in my mouth.* I have
learned that when praises go up, blessings come down!

Now no doubt there were some women, like some people
in our congregations today, who did not think all that was
necessary. *It doesn't take all of that*, they probably say! They
thought Miriam was out of place and that she had taken this thing
a little too far. They thought that the singing and the timbrels and
the dancing were not necessary. In fact, they might have even
said, *Why couldn't they simply bow down and pray a prayer of
thanksgiving?*

But, I can see Miriam working the crowd—compelling
them to give God the glory and all the honor. Miriam understood
full well the miracle that God had performed for Israel by
opening the Red Sea for them to walk through and then drowning
Pharaoh's army. God had spared their lives. And in response to
God's goodness, Miriam took out her tambourine and started
praising God.

I have learned that praise is contagious! Miriam gave her
own testimony. She probably said, *Praying might be good
enough for you; coming to worship and acting reverent might be
good enough for you; but you don't know like I know, what the
Lord has done for me. You were not there when he saved my
soul; you were not there when he renewed my hope; when he
healed my body; when he saved my life. You don't know like I
know, what the Lord has done for me!* Miriam knew that praying
was good, but she also knew that praying does'n take the place of
praise. She even wrote a beautiful Psalm about the Lord's

marvelous works. She just had to open her mouth. She just had to say to the Lord, *Thank you!*

Miriam could serve God because she had learned how to praise the Lord. She loved God, and was not ashamed to praise Him. She lifted up her voice before the Lord and made a joyful noise unto Him. She was a woman after God's own heart. And if you and I want to be used of the Lord, we had better first learn how to submit and surrender our will and our way unto the Him. We had better first learn how to unashamedly praise Him. You see, Miriam was a woman of praise.

I don't know how you feel about praise, but it is not difficult for me to praise God. All I have to do is think of God's goodness, think of God's love, think of God's Mercy, and I can't help but offer praise. I simply think about how God has not given me what I *really* deserve, but has had mercy on me. *When I think of the goodness of Jesus, and all he's done for me, my soul cries out 'hallelujah' I thank God for saving me.*

Miriam, A Jealous And Rebellious Woman

Miriam was a woman of praise and a woman of prophecy, but before they got to the promised land of Canaan, we see her in the midst of a family feud. She became a jealous and rebellious woman.

In order to understand how such a drastic change could take place in Miriam, we must understand that in the beginning and throughout his life, Miriam had been Moses' "big sister;" she was Moses' "protector," if you will. You will remember from the book of Exodus, that it was Miriam who anxiously and purposefully watched Moses float down the Nile river in the bassinet made of bulrushes, until the Pharaoh's daughter rescued him. Then Miriam rushed over to give assistance; she told the Egyptian girl that she had a Hebrew woman who could be a wet nurse for the baby. Miriam was accustomed to looking out for her brother, Moses.

So she became jealous when Moses married a Cushite woman, an Ethiopian woman—a "sister girl"—by the name of Ziporah. Before Ziporah, Moses had always depended on Miriam; she had kept a watchful eye over him in the Pharaoh's house. But the bible says that Moses ran off and got married. Miriam was obviously jealous. My sisters, let me remind you that jealousy is a green-eyed monster and envy is her twin sister!

The text before us says: *And Miriam and Aaron began to talk against Moses because of his Cushite wife, for he had married a Cushite.* It is important to note whose name is listed first in this text—Miriam. This means that she was the leader of this sedition. She said, *Has the Lord spoken only through Moses? Hasn't He also spoken through us?* Well, I see a warning here for someone. You may think that you're on a private line when you get on the telephone and start putting down your pastors or criticizing the church leadership. Well, the story of Miriam and Aaron is useful for reminding us that God is always the third party. The Bible says that *the Lord heard them*!

Now, we shouldn't forget that the family feud was about two things. Miriam was jealous of Moses' wife. Not only that, she was jealous of Moses' position with God because God spoke to Moses face to face. God always responded to Moses when Moses interceded on behalf of the people. God held back plagues; God stopped judgements; God gave them chance after chance after chance *because* Moses interceded on behalf of the Israelites. Moses was in God's face day and night, night and day, pleading for mercy for the people in the camp.

Moses was their leader called by God at the burning bush. And it is a good thing because you will remember the mess Aaron made when Moses left him in charge while he went to Mount Sinai to receive the law from God. Aaron proved himself to be an ineffective leader. Aaron instructed the people to take off their gold, and he made a golden calf for the people to worship and then he blamed the people: *Moses, you know the people, that they are bent on evil.*

But Aaron had followed the people rather than leading them. Leaders are commissioned to lead, to take authority. But Aaron failed in his task, and then lied by saying that the people forced him to build a false image. Aaron could not even stand the heat for a few days, yet Aaron and Miriam wanted to be in charge because they thought they could do the job better than Moses.

The sedition of Miriam and Aaron shows us that jealousy will always lead to rebellion. Miriam wanted to take the lead. Notice that the Bible said that Miriam led the women in praise. But just because you are good at one thing does not mean you can handle the whole ship. In today's vernacular, she was a ministerial staff person, but she wanted to be the pastor.

Miriam thought she could handle the entire camp. And surely she could do a better job than Moses was doing. Do you know anybody like that? Have you ever had a thought like that?

Perhaps, God should have given Miriam the reigns for a while, and allowed her to see first hand what it is like to be in charge of the entire camp. A camp full of mumbling, grumbling, complaining, ungrateful, unfaithful people like these Israelites. Miriam was envious; this lead to jealously, which led to rebellion. We need to stop envying other people's churches, other people's positions.

Miriam thought more highly of herself than she ought to have thought. She thought she was "all that!" Some of us are like that in the church today. Always wanting somebody else's church, somebody else's job, or somebody else's position in the church, community, or government.

But if you know like I know, you had better go ahead and do the best job you can with what the Lord has given you because you may not be able to handle the entire camp. Miriam didn't know Moses' agony. She was probably sleeping while Moses was praying, resting while he was pacing the floor trying to deal with getting this entire camp of unruly, unfaithful people to the safety of Canaan. Miriam thought too much of herself and ended up jealous and rebellious.

Consequences Of Jealousy And Rebellion

Miriam and Aaron seemed to forget that God is Sovereign. By challenging Moses' authority, they actually challenged God's authority; and by doing so, they brought the judgement of God on themselves. As Numbers 12:9 tells us, *The anger of the Lord burned against them, and He left them.* And now we see the judgement of God.

Miriam and Aaron had overstepped their bounds. She thought more highly of herself than she ought; she because puffed up; she forgot her place; she wanted to take Moses' place. So she rebelled. But remember that the consequences of rebellion are always judgement!

Now notice that Moses, the pastor, did not have to say a word to Miriam or Aaron; God dealt with them directly. I tell you, if you hold your peace and let the Lord fight your battles, victory will be yours.

The Bible says that when the cloud lifted from above the tent, there stood Miriam—leprous like snow. Just look at Miriam now—cast out of the camp; forbidden to fellowship; forbidden to serve. She doesn't look like a woman after God's own heart now! She is not praising God now; she is not dancing now; she is not singing; she's not even a leader now. Just look at her now—she is a pitiful leprous wreck, all because of jealously and rebellion.

The Bible says that as soon as Aaron turned toward her and saw that she had leprosy—saw the judgement of God on her—he started pleading his case to Moses for himself and for Miriam. *Please, my Lord, do not hold against us this sin we have so foolishly committed. Do not let her be like a stillborn infant coming from it's mother's womb with it's flesh half eaten away.*

Aaron was begging for mercy because he realized that his and their arms were too short to box with God. The lesson—don't ever think more highly of yourself than you ought!

Don't Leave Without Miriam

Miriam learned from the Red Sea experience that God was a deliverer, that God was a miracle worker because He had parted the Red Sea and allowed them to walk through on dry land while the enemy drowned, and in that same Red Sea. But here, Miriam learns another lesson.

This woman of God learns that God is not only a deliverer, He is not only able to work miracles in our lives. She learns that God is gracious and merciful. The Bible tells us that *Miriam was struck with leprosy, and Miriam was shut out from the camp seven days. And the people journeyed not till Miriam was brought in again.*

Do you see what I see? Look again at the text. It says, *And the people journeyed not till Miriam was brought in again.* I Do you see the mercy of God? I also see the mercy that God expects His children to have for one another. The camp did no move for seven days; they refused to leave Miriam behind; they realized that Miriam was not completely lost. Miriam was down but she was not out; cast down but not forsaken—they never gave up on Miriam. Rather, they interceded; they fasted and they prayed for her return.

Not only did the camp realize that Miriam was down but not out, but here Miriam realizes that the God she loves and serves is a merciful God! God could have killed her; God could have told the camp to leave her behind; God could have let her live the rest of her days suffering the dreaded disease of leprosy. But instead, God executed mercy rather than justice. The punishment was only temporary.

Some of the people probably wanted to leave Miriam and said, *It's her own fault! She brought it on herself. Good enough for her. Why should we stay around here waiting for her? She always thought she was better than all the other women!* Well, thank God, "they" were not in charge. Thank God that Moses, the leader, the one she had rebelled against, was truly a God-fearing man; a humble and a merciful man. Someone had the sense to shout out, *Wait, we cannot go yet!*

Well, there are still too many of us all still outside the camp! We cannot all run to the suburbs and forget the inner city; our blood is in the inner city! We cannot desert our own by thinking we are better than they are. We can't go yet! We cannot write our young people off! I see them on the street corners doing and dealing drugs; being destroyed by drugs, hating themselves and hating one another which leads to killing one another. So we can't go yet! They are a part of us! That's some deacon's daughter outside the camp! *We can't go yet!*

If we desert them, they will all be lost. And Jesus would that none should be lost. We must learn to follow Aaron's and Moses' lead! We must plead for our brothers and sisters! We must take them to the throne of grace! Look for the fallen; wait for the fallen. Do not be so satisfied that you are saved or that you forget about everybody around you.

The camp can't move: *Miriam is still outside the camp!*

After Miriam came back in, then, the camp moved on. When God is merciful in your life, you ought to praise Him all the more. We thought Miriam knew how to praise God before, when God delivered Israel from Egypt's bondage. But I'm sure that was nothing compared to what Miriam did when she was ushered back into the camp—back into the fellowship of the saints.

I'm sure she ran awhile! I'm sure she danced awhile! I'm sure she sang awhile! I'm sure she sang awhile! I'm sure she played her tambourine like never before. Miriam had a new song to sing! She had a new testimony to give; she knew first hand the boundless love of God. Can't you just hear Miriam singing:

> *You can't make me doubt him;*
> *You can't make me doubt him;*
> *You can't make me doubt him in my heart.*
> *You can't make me doubt him;*
> *I know too much about him;*
> *You can't make me doubt him in my heart.*

THE MIRIAM SYNDROME
Numbers 12:1;15-16

STUDY QUESTIONS

1. Miriam had a song of praise that she led the Israelites in singing. What New Testament female also had a song of praise and where is it located in the Bible?

2. If the camp waited seven days for Miriam before they left, why is it that we often find it difficult to wait on other people to get saved or to develop a personal relationship with God?

3. This message shows that God will use anyone who makes his or her life available to Him. Since Miriam was being used by God as a protector of Moses, praise leader, and prophetess, what would cause her to become jealous and rebellious of Moses?

4. Some biblical scholars believe Miriam spoke against Moses because he married Ziporah, a Cushite. What evidence is there that Miriam expressed feelings of prejudice/jealousy or both?

5. How does Miriam compare with female ministers serving under a pastor?

6. What rebellious traits have you seen in your own church?

CHAPTER VII

FAITH MAKES THE DIFFERENCE

Numbers 13:30-33

And Caleb stilled the people before Moses, and said, Let us go up at once, and possess it; for we are able to overcome it. 31 But the men that went up with him said, be not able to go up against the people; for they are stronger than we. 32 And they brought up an evil report of the land which they had searched unto the children of Israel, saying, The land, through which we have gone to search it, is a land that eateth up the inhabitants thereof; and all the people that we saw in it are men of a great stature. 33 And there we saw the giants, the sons of Anak, which come of the giants: and we were in our own sight as grasshoppers, and so we were in their sight.

Throughout the history of Israel, God's chosen people had a faith problem. At the Red Sea experience, they wanted to return to slavery. They mumbled, *Moses brought us here to die. We could have stayed in Egypt.* In the wilderness, they did not trust God for food and water. Again they mumbled, *"We are going to starve to death; at least we had food to eat in Egypt."*

When they reached the border of Canaan, they still complained, *We be not able to go up against the people, for they are stronger than we.* It was all because they lacked faith. I want to suggest that Israel's greatest downfall was, in fact, her lack of faith. She simply did not believe the promises of God.

I want to remind you that on this Christian journey, it is our faith that makes the difference. Such is the case in our text.

As the people of God reach the long sought after Promised Land, after all that God had brought them through, they yet lacked faith.

Look with me at how our text speaks to us and shows us three things about the power of faith.

Faith Makes The Difference In What You See And How You Perceive What You See.

You will notice from the text that both groups saw the same things physically. They saw giants, walled cities, strong men and humongous bunches of fruit. But Caleb and Joshua had a different perspective about what they saw. The difference was based on the fact that they saw with eyes of faith, while the ten spies saw only with their natural eyes. So the faithless ten brought back an evil report.

The faithless ten saw only stumbling blocks, they saw only obstacles; they saw only defeat, they saw only discouragement—they said *we are not able to take the land.* Joshua and Caleb saw the same things that the other ten spies saw, but they perceived them differently!

Why?

Because one group looked with eyes of faith and the other looked with the eyes of fear. Fear sees obstacles, but faith sees opportunities. Fear sees problems, but faith sees possibilities. The language of fear is *we cannot take the land* but the language of faith is *we are well able to take it.* The language of fear is *we cannot make a difference in the problems our communities face.*

The problem of teenage pregnancy; the problem of school drop-outs; the problem of Black-on-Black crime; the problem of the break-up of our Black families; the problem of the relentless flow of drugs in our communities and on our college campuses; the ever present problems of racism, all speak in the language of fear.

It says, *We be not able to go up against the people; for they are stronger than we. We can not take the land.* But the language of faith is *give me this mountain... with God, all things are possible!*

The ten spies looked at the stature of the men who inhabited the land; they looked at the strong walls around the city; they looked at the size even of the crops that they grew—grapes so large that they had to place them on poles to carry them. They only saw what their 20/20 vision allowed them to see. Their main problem was that they forgot who it was that promised them the land. They forgot who it was that sent them in to spy out the land. They forgot about the Lord in the equation of who was stronger than whom! They forgot that God plus one is a majority. Better still, that God alone is a majority. They forgot Leviticus 26:8, which reads:

> *And five of you shall chase an hundred,*
> *and an hundred of you shall put ten*
> *thousand to flight; and your enemies shall*
> *fall before you by the sword.*

They forgot that God knew what was in the land before God ever sent them to check it out. God knew what the deal was; God had the battle plan all mapped out. In God's eyes, the battle was fought and the victory was won until they put their mouths in it! You and I *ought to keep* our mouths out of God's affairs. If God said it, that ought to settle it for us. Ten of the spies took their eyes off of the Almighty God and started looking at their own inadequacies. They forgot about the power of God to fight for them; they began to depend on their own power. They forgot that *if I hold my peace and let the Lord fight my battles, victory, victory will be mine!*

Faith makes the difference in how you perceive what you see. So Caleb and Joshua had no problem with the giants, or the strength of the men, or the strong walls because they understood from the beginning that they came in the name of the Lord. If the Lord be for you, what is the whole world against you? It was their faith that made the difference in what they saw.

Why?

Because one group understood that the battle was not theirs, that the battle belongs to the Lord! We need to understand that no matter what it looks like to the physical eye; no matter what your intellect tells you, if God said you can have the land, the land belongs to you. If God said you can have the job, it's yours. I don't care how much more qualified the other applicants are, you walk into corporate America's headquarters with your head held high, shoulders back, a confident smile on your Black face and simply ask: *When do I start*? If God said you can do it, write the proposal to start your own business and take it to the bank.

When you get there, ask the manager: *What's the lowest interest rate you have?* If you can believe God, you can receive it. Faith makes the difference!

Faith Makes The Difference In How You See Yourself And How Others See You

The problem with most Christians is that we think far too little of ourselves. We, like the Israelites, have grasshopper mentalities. We think everybody else is stronger and greater than we. We underestimate ourselves. We forget what the Bible says about who we are and what we can do. We forget that *greater is He that is in us than he than he that is in the world.* We forget that *we are more than conquerors through Him that loves us.* We forget that *five of you shall chase an hundred, and an hundred of you shall put ten thousand to flight.*

We forget that *at the name of Jesus, every knee shall bow and every tongue confess that Jesus Christ is Lord.* We also forget that if we *resist the devil, he will flee from us.* We forget that Jesus said, *greater things than these shall you yet do in my name.* We forget that we serve a risen Savior and neither death, nor hell, nor the grave could hold Jesus down. He got up on the third day, and because He got up with all power in His hands, there is no power in earth—Republican or Democrat—or in hell

that can hold us down. *No weapon formed against us shall prosper. I can do all things, through Christ who strengthens me!*
The problem with the ten spies, and the problem with our people today is that we think too little of ourselves! The ten spies who brought the evil report said out of their own mouths.

> *The land, through which we have gone to search is a land that eateth up the inhabitants... and all the people that we saw in it are men of a great stature ... and we were in our own sight as grasshoppers, and so we were in their sight.*
> —Numbers 13:32-33

We must also understand that the Israelites had defeated these men earlier in their journey. Rahab told the two spies that the people of Jericho trembled at word of what God had done with the Israelites at the Red Sea, and that they were afraid of them coming their way. The Israelites called themselves grasshoppers, but the enemy was afraid of the Israelites!
They clearly had no faith in themselves or their God. They were openly declaring that these men were stronger and more powerful than God's people. As if that wasn't bad enough, they put themselves down.
They said *and to ourselves, we seemed like grasshoppers, and so we seemed to them.* The Israelites thought too little of themselves.
In Proverbs 23:7, Solomon says, *As a man thinketh in his heart, so is he.* One of our problems as a people is that too many of us think of ourselves as little *grasshoppers.*
Black History Month is a wonderful effort to bring to our consciousness the reality of what a great people African-Americans are. But Black History Month is not enough. Too many of our youth have not been taught that they are the sons and daughters of Africa, the sons and daughters of kings and queens—of warriors and builders of nations—the sons and

daughters of inventors of math and the first physicians. Our children need to know that Europeans, as we know them, stole our math and science formulas and claimed them as their own. Our young people need to be clear that America was built on the blood, sweat, and tears of *Black folk*—Black folk who did not ask to come to this country. Black people who were already leaders of civilized nations. We can raise the self-esteem of our young people by reminding them that our forefathers built colleges and institutions of higher learning when it was against the law for them to learn to read and write themselves.

They didn't have six figure salaries, but former slaves built universities like Howard, Hampton and Wilberforce Universities so that you and I could have what all too many of them were denied—an education to prepare us to become capable leaders of this nation—since they wanted us here so badly in the first place! Our people must use not just February, but every opportunity to lift up the achievements of our fore parents and Blacks in our society who are achievers and over-achievers. Because the truth of the matter is that we have to first come from behind before we can even get out in front of those who have been given every privilege possible.

We must understand that just because we live, or lived, in the ghetto, we don't have to live with a ghetto mentality. There is a difference in being poor economically and being poor in spirit. Poverty never held our foreparents back. Black folk know how to make it in poverty, but the poor in spirit can't make it because they lack hope; they lack foresight; they lack integrity; they lack self-determination—the kind of determination which Langston Hughes described when he wrote, *life for me ain't been no crystal stair... but I keeps on a climbing."*

Because the ten spies did not think highly of themselves, they automatically thought that the inhabitants of the land thought nothing of them. Whether or not you've realized it yet, that's what a lack of faith will do. But when you have faith in God, no uncircumcised Philistine; no Hittite; no Perizzite; no

Jebusite; no Canaanite; no giant is too big for you to go up against.

Faith Makes The Difference In The Outcome
Of The Situation

When we had nothing else, we had the Lord. Whether we were slaves or Colored, or Negro, or Black, or African-American, we never got our *forty acres and a mule*. But we held on to God's unchanging hand because we knew how to *steal away and have a little talk with Jesus;* somehow, we made it this far by faith.

I want us to remember that even in the dark days ahead, faith will make the difference in the outcome of your situation. Times are going to get harder than they are if certain republicans get their way, but we can win the battle if we trust God. Faith makes the difference in how you see yourself—a grasshopper or a giant.

If you don't believe me, then ask a little shepherd boy named David. The fiercest giant in the land—one named Goliath—who had tormented Saul's army with fear, made the mistake of threatening a boy half his nine-foot size. He teased David; he laughed at little David's stature; but David met him face to face because faith makes the difference.

David said: *How dare you defy the army of the living God! You may be bigger than I, but I come in the name of the Lord... The Lord is my light and my salvation, whom shall I fear; the Lord is the strength of my life, of whom shall I be afraid; when the wicked, even my enemies, came up against me to eat up my flesh, they stumbled and fell. Though an host should encamp against me, my heart shall not fear. For in the time of trouble, He shall hide me in His pavilion, in the secret of His tabernacle shall He hide me. He shall set me upon a rock and now shall my head be lifted up above mine enemy.*

David had killed the lion and the bear by the power of God. David was not afraid of Goliath because David understood that he had the power of God with him!

It's not about who's stronger or who's more powerful; who's more skilled or the color of your skin, the texture of your hair. It's not about who has more economic power, which way the scales of justice are tilted or whether you are the majority or the minority! *If God be for you*, who in the whole world can be against you? Our hard fought for civil rights laws have been watered down, affirmative action is all but history. But, my friends, hold on. God always has the last word!

You may feel like a grasshopper!

You may feel out-numbered!

You may feel less powerful!

But if you hold your peace and let the Lord fight your battle, victory shall be yours *because* you belong to the Lord.

Goliath was nine feet tall and had a sword and shield; all David had was a slingshot and five smooth stones. But he came in the name of the Lord.

He came in faith!

Faith made the difference!

All we have is faith, determination and integrity; but we come in the name of the Lord!

The problem we have is the same problem that the ten spies had!

They forgot who they were and whose they were!

They forgot that God had promised to give them this land flowing with milk and honey!

They forgot that God was on their side!

They forgot that they came in the name of the Lord!

Education doesn't take the place of having the Lord on your side!

Degrees and letters are no substitute for faith in God. Get all the education you can, but don't forget the Lord. It was the Lord who brought us thus far. Those who trusted in God entered the Promised Land; the others perished.

Where is your trust?

Is your faith in self or the Almighty God?

God told the Israelites that for everyday that they spent spying out the land, they would spend a year in the wilderness.

Why?

Because they doubted God's word.

Why?

Because they doubted God's power.

Faith makes the difference.

Now what do you believe?

Do you believe that God can do anything?

Do you even believe that God can save your life from a dying hell?

Do you believe that God can transform your life and make it worth living?

Do you believe that God can change your situation?

Do you believe that God can deliver you?

What you believe depends on your faith!

Where you spend eternity depends on your faith!

FAITH MAKES THE DIFFERENCE!

FAITH MAKES THE DIFFERENCES
Numbers 13:30-33

STUDY QUESTIONS

1. Recall a time when you were in a situation that appeared overwhelming. What biblical characters' behavior represents how you responded?

2. Find ten scriptures that mention or deal with faith. Which ones have ministered to you in times of doubt?

3. If you had to leave behind a FAITH LAST WILL AND TESTAMENT for your children, what would you say about the importance of believing in the promises of God despite difficult circumstances?

4. For the next seven days, write down the number of times you make statements that include words of doubt and words of faith. Which list is longer?

5. Make a list of seven scriptures that describe the importance of faith. Would you be willing to learn one a day?

CHAPTER VIII

A DIFFERENT SPIRIT

Numbers 14:24

But my servant Caleb, because he had another spirit with him, and hath followed me fully, him will I bring into the land where into he went; and his seed shall possess it.

What Made Caleb's Spirit Different?

S ome people pride themselves on being like everyone else. They follow the crowd. They have no ideals of their own. They have no plans or agendas of their own. They are content simply to follow the crowd. They have no convictions of their own. The obvious problem with these kinds of people is that the crowd is not always on the right track, which is clearly demonstrated in the text from which this sermon is taken.

This man, Caleb, was singled out by God, not because he followed the crowd, but because he was different. The text said:

But my servant Caleb, because he had another spirit with him, and hath followed me fully...

Caleb was singled out because he was different.

Having a different spirit really has nothing to do with how you look, or how you walk, or anything physical. It has more to do with your outlook on life. It is how you think about things. Caleb was an optimist, not a pessimist. When he looked at a situation he did not see defeat; he saw an opportunity for God to perform a miracle. What and how you see things has a direct correlation to your thought processes. In fact, the Bible says, *as a man thinketh so is he.* Caleb saw victory and that made him a winner. He had a different spirit, one that said, *with God all things are possible.* He had a spirit that said, *I can do all things through Christ which strengthens me.* That's the exact kind of spirit that God desires in His people.

Although Caleb saw the same things the others witnessed, Caleb was able to give a different report because he had an active faith and a living spirit within him. He did not suffer from what the other spies had—spiritual amnesia.

They forgot about Egypt and the hard taskmasters.

They forgot about the plagues.

They forgot about the pillar of cloud by day and fire by night.

They seemed to have forgotten about the Red Sea, manna from heaven, and the bitter water turning sweet.

They forgot all of the miracles that God worked through God's servant Moses.

They simply said, *we had it better in Egypt.*

But this faith-crippling ailment did not afflict Caleb. Caleb remembered the goodness of the Lord and said along with Joshua, *We are well able.* One's faith is activated when one remembers God's goodness. That is what is called *having a different spirit.* God is clearly looking for people who have a different spirit.

In order to understand Caleb better, it is important to know that Caleb came from the tribe of Judah. The word "Judah" means "praise the Lord." So Caleb was a praise warrior and not a pessimistic murmurer. Caleb learned through his up-bringing that in the face of insurmountable odds, praise is the best defense. That is exactly what God expects from us when facing the devastating ailments that face our communities today. Praise unto God is appropriate when dealing with AIDS patients or cancer patients, with Black-on-Black crime, with sexism, with racism, with teenage pregnancy, with the mean spirited conservative trend in our country.

Praise can change a situation from negative to positive. Praise calls God's attention to the matter.

Praise breaks through the atmosphere straight up to the stratosphere into the very courts of heaven and demands God's immediate attention. God inhabits the praises of Israel. Caleb was a man who knew how to praise the Lord.

> Praise will replace your doubts with determination!
> Praise will change your hopelessness into hopefulness!
> Praise will change your sorrow into joy!
> Praise will replace your fear with faith!
> Praise will turn your midnights into day!
> Praise will turn your mountains into molehills!
> Praise will take you out of self and place you in the right spirit!
> Praise will make demons tremble.

Caleb was from the tribe of Judah—a tribe that was founded on praising the Lord.

How To Get A Different Spirit

The bible is replete with examples of how we can change our lives from negative to positive in the Lord.

David is a prime example. David prayed for *a different spirit*. After the prophet Nathan reminded David of his horrible sin of adultery and murder, David prayed. David prayed because he recognized that he was out of the will of God. When you truly have a heart for God, when you truly love God, you can no longer casually sin and not be convicted by it. You will realize that you need *a different spirit*. It hurts you when you know you have offended the one you love, the one who loves you. That's why David prayed the infamous prayer in Psalms 51:10-12:

> *Create in me a clean heart, O God; and*
> *renew a right spirit within me. Cast me not*
> *away from thy presence; and take not thy holy*

spirit from me. Restore unto me the joy of thy
salvation; and uphold me with thy free spirit.

Caleb's spirit was different because he was a man of praise and he had unshakable faith in the Lord. David was also a man of praise. But David had a different spirit because of his steadfast love and faith in the Lord. David never turned back on God. David trusted God when he fought the giant Goliath; he could be heard saying, *I come in the name of the living God.* He never once said or implied that he came on his own strength or might.

David's life demonstrates for us that God lets us know when our sprits get out of line. We serve a confidential God. God will send you word—often through the prophet of God—to let you know that it is time to straighten up and fly right.

That is often what is happening when you accuse the preacher of "stepping on your toes" during the sermon. It's not actually the preacher but rather, your "Nathan" that is letting you know that it's time for renewal, it's time for revival, it's time for repentance; it's time to renew your spirit and get right with God.

Caleb's Different Spirit

Unlike Caleb you might not have been born into a praise family. Your father might not have been a preacher. Your mother might not have been a missionary. Maybe your grandmother did not love the name of Jesus. But you can be born again spiritually into the praise family of God.

God said, *My servant Caleb, because he had a different spirit with him and hath followed me fully...*

From the beginning of the search through the 40 days, Caleb was faithful. In the end, he brought back a good report. Caleb lived in the camp of Israel for 45 years and he never murmured or complained with the other Israelites. Caleb did not claim his heritage until age 85; but the good old man was still following faithfully. Caleb lived to enter the Promised Land after the 40 years had passed, and all because he had a different spirit.

Caleb was different because he was willing to carry the big sweet grapes; but he was also willing to fight the big giants. All too many of God's servants ask to be excused from the hard jobs but want to have the sweet duties.

We don't volunteer to go to the mission fields.

We don't volunteer to visit the sick and imprisoned.

We don't volunteer to house the homeless and clothe the naked.

We don't volunteer to pastor in the far and remote places.

We, like the Israelites, want to carry the sweet grapes, but we do not want to fight the giants. One of the safest tests of sincerity is found in a willingness to suffer for the cause.

Caleb had a different spirit because he followed cheerfully without disputing; he followed constantly without declining; he followed sincerely and was no hypocrite.

Caleb had a different spirit because he followed with his whole heart.

How To Maintain A Right Spirit

The condition of your spirit will determine how everything in your life operates. We must guard our spirits and not allow them to become contaminated with things of the world—things like hatred, fear, lust, greed, lying, doubting, bitterness and being unforgiving. Not only that, but we must be careful of those with whom we associate. Association has been known to promote assimilation. We need people of faith in our lives if we are going to be encouraged to stay on the right track.

If we would be effective servants of the Most High King, we must maintain a right spirit. If we would remain faithful, we must maintain a right spirit. We cannot serve the Lord effectively with a lot of worldly baggage weighing us down. We, like Caleb, must be a people of praise; and like David, we must be a people of prayer in order to maintain a right spirit. We can never maintain our right spirit solely on our own strength. Our praise must be consistent. Our prayer life must be consistent. We must constantly ask the Lord to "fill my cup ..."

Please understand that God knows what kind of spirit you and I have. That's why God turned the Israelites around to wander in the wilderness for 40 years. That's why God sent Nathan to David for correction. That's why God commended Caleb on his *different spirit.* If we would be pleasing unto the Lord, we must be careful to maintain a right spirit.

Well, spirits, like most things in life, need to be renewed every now and then. The best made car has to have regular servicing. A red light comes on to indicate that service is needed. The manufacturer schedules them for regular tune-ups—to check everything out—to make sure all of the parts are operating properly. If an automobile needs to be regulated, surely your spirit and my spirit needs to be renewed on a regular basis. That's why prayer is so important.

> *Search me, O God, and know my Heart; try me, and*
> *know my thoughts:*
> *And see if there be any wicked way in me, and lead me*
> *in the way everlasting.*
> —Psalms 139:23-24

> *Purge me with hyssop, and I shall be clean: wash me,*
> *and I shall be whiter than* snow.
> —Psalms 51:7

David prayed because he recognized that he was out of the will of God; David was simply guarding his spirit. King David was humble enough to admit his wrong and had enough sense to go before the Lord and repent and ask for a right spirit.

You and I can afford to do no less than King David. When we see our spirits getting out of line, when the red light comes on, we must go before the Lord and ask for a right spirit.

*Create in me a clean heart, O God; and renew a
right spirit within me.
Cast me not away from thy presence; and take not thy
holy spirit from me.
Restore unto me the joy of thy Salvation; and uphold me
with thy free spirit.*

—Psalms 51:10-12

Ultimately, it is only God who can give us a right spirit!

It is only God, our creator, who knows how to make the wrongs in our lives right!

I'm a living witness that God is not only able, but God is willing to *renew a right spirit within us.*

All we need is *A DIFFERENT SPIRIT*!

A DIFFERENT SPIRIT
Numbers 14:24

STUDY QUESTIONS

1. What does it mean to have "a different spirit" and how can you attain this goal?

2. What are three examples of behavior that indicates someone having a "different spirit" that is ungodly?

3. Looking back at the message, what practical ways are provided to help you and others maintain a "right spirit?"

4. What are three examples of behavior that suggests someone having a "different spirit" that is godly?

5. Caleb followed God cheerfully regardless of how situations appeared in his life. What other evidence is there in the message that Caleb had a *different spirit*?

CHAPTER IX

TRUST AND OBEY

Numbers 14:6-10

And Joshua the son of Nun, and Caleb the son of Jephunneh, which were of them that searched the land, rent their clothes: 7 And they spake unto all the company of the children of Israel, saying, The land, which we passed through to search it, is an exceeding good land. 8 If the LORD delight in us, then he will bring us into the land, and give it us; a land which floweth with milk and honey. 9 Only rebel not ye against the LORD, neither fear ye the people of the land; for they are bread for us: their defence is departed from them, and the LORD is with us: fear them not. 10 But all the congregation bade stone them with stones. And the glory of the LORD appeared in the tabernacle of the congregation before all the children of Israel.

When a believer says he or she trusts God, it means having faith in God. Faith, as the Bible describes it in Hebrews 11:1, is *knowing that something is real even if we do not see it.* To obey basically means to follow instructions—to do what we are told. The Bible teaches us to be "doers" of the Word, and not hearers only. The Bible tells us to *keep the Lord's commandments to do them.* Every believer needs to understand that trusting and obeying do not necessarily go hand in hand. They should, but trusting is not necessarily obeying. Trusting is the confession of one's faith: but obeying is the acting out of one's faith. The Bible says that *faith without works is dead.* But all too many Christians never get past the *"confession"* stage of their faith to the obeying of God's word. The subject is *Trust and Obey.*

Joshua and Caleb were trying to persuade the Israelites to trust and to obey the Lord. They knew full well the odds they were up against. They, too, had entered Canaan and spied out the land, and had seen the giants. They saw the walled cities. They saw that the city was well fortified. They saw the size of the fruit of the land. They understood full well that physically, the land was out of their reach, but that by faith they could take it, because the Lord had assured them of it. This is the land God had promised to their forefathers, Abraham, Isaac and Jacob. God brought them out of Egypt's slavery to give them this land—a land flowing with milk and honey. Canaan was to be their "heaven on earth." Canaan was to be their inheritance—a city with houses they had not built; a city with walls they had not constructed; a city with bountiful crops that they had not planted. God's intention and His desire was to give it to them.

Because of their lack of faith, they were afraid to take the land. They brought an evil report to the people of God. They said: *Moses brought us out here to die; God could have left us in Egypt. These giants will devour us.* But Joshua and Caleb persisted in their faith. *The land we passed through and explored is exceedingly good. If the Lord is pleased. He will lead us into that land—a land flowing with milk and honey—and will give it to us.*

Joshua and Caleb warned the Israelites, *Do not rebel against the Lord; do not be afraid of the people of the land; we will swallow them up. Their protection is good, but the Lord is with us. Do not be afraid of them.*

Joshua and Caleb were trying to persuade them to *"trust and obey"* the Lord their God.

Because we often find ourselves in the predicament of the ten spies—too fearful to trust and obey—I have a few suggestions on: *How to obey in spite of the odds.*

Never Allow Your Confusion To Disrupt Your Obedience

Too often, if we don't understand a situation, if we can't see the end result of a situation, if we can't analyze it, figure it out to the ninth degree, then we won't trust God in that situation. Actually, that's not trusting God at all. If you know the result; if you can see the end, then faith or trust is not needed. Remember that *faith is knowing that something is real even though we do not see it.*

Abraham was confused about sacrificing his only son Isaac, but he did not allow confusion to disrupt his obedience. We know the story of Abraham and how he trusted God when he didn't know why. He did not understand why God asked him to sacrifice the son of promise, the son he had to wait until he was 99 years old to produce, the son about whom he boasted, the son upon whom he depended to carry his name and produce a great nation.

Abraham had to have been confused about God's motives, about why God would ask such a hard thing of him. He did not know why, but he did not allow his confusion to block his obedience. He took Isaac to Mount Moriah, and was fully prepared to sacrifice his only son. Abraham found out that God's name is Jehovah Jireh—God who provides. God provided a lamb to take Isaac's place. Abraham had obeyed God against all odds.

Noah must have been confused about the need to build an ark on dry land with no rain clouds in sight, without a promise of financing for the project. But, he obeyed God. Mary and Joseph were confused about a virgin birth, but they trusted and obeyed God's plan for their lives. Never allow your confusion to disrupt your obedience.

Never Be Swayed By What You See With Your Natural Eyes

They saw giants; they saw walled cities; they saw humongous crops; they saw well-fortified cities. Ten were swayed saying, *and to ourselves we seemed like grasshoppers, and so we seemed to them.* But the two faithful spies, Joshua and

Caleb, did not allow what they saw to overrule what they knew. They knew that God was greater than any enemy. They had not forgotten what God had already done for them at the Red Sea and in the wilderness. When you have a history with God, you can step out on nothing and expect everything, because you know for yourself what God can do.

We know the story of the lad with two small fish and five barley loaves—they saw over 5,000 hungry men (not including the women and children) fed. The disciples allowed human nature to get in the way—*but what are these among so many?* They forgot that God was in the equation. They forgot that when a little is placed in God's hand, it becomes enough! We can't afford to look at circumstances with our natural eyes. We must learn to live with eyes of faith—eyes that see the supernatural working of the God we love and serve.

Remember That God Stands By His Word And His Promises
God had already proven that He could be trusted.

- God brought them out of Egypt!
- God parted the Red Sea and allowed the Israelites to walk through on dry land while Pharaoh's army drowned!
- God sent manna from heaven during their journey in the wilderness!
- God brought water out of dry places when they were thirsty in the desert!
- God fulfilled His promise to be with them always—a pillar of cloud by day and a pillar of fire by night!
- God gave them victory over their enemies when they were obedient!
- God brought them safely through the wilderness!
- God kept clothes on their backs, shoes on their feet and shelter over their heads!

- God brought them to the boarder of Canaan!

Now that they were at the borders of Canaan, what made them think that God could not give them the Promised Land? What makes you think God can't do what He promised to do in your life? The problem is that we forget too quickly what God has already done. We forgot how He got us through the last Red Sea. We forgot how He rescued us from the last storm. We forgot how He provided for us when we were out of a job; how He got us out of a sick bed; how He delivered us form a life threatening habit; how He helped us raise unruly children; how He kept that rocky marriage intact; how he opened a door that no man could open.

Based upon what God has already done, we ought to trust and obey. But like the unfaithful Israelites, we are quick to forget God's past blessings; we are afraid to step out on faith. We are afraid to bring a real *first fruits offering,* a real sacrificial offering, because we think we won't have enough for ourselves. We want to build a church, but we are afraid to trust and obey God's word by bringing the whole tithe into the storehouse of the Lord. We seem to be afraid to serve God with our whole heart. Yet God has given us salvation. It was guaranteed when God said: *If thou shalt confess with thou mouth the Lord Jesus, and believe in thine heart that God has raised Jesus from the dead, thou shalt be saved.*

It is worth repeating that the word *trust* is defined as having faith in something or someone or having confidence in something or someone. It means to believe or to depend on something future or contingent. In other words to trust is to have hope. When a believers say they trust God that is the same as saying that they have faith in God.

Faith is suppose to be an action word for Christians, but all too many of us never get pass the *"confession"* stage of our faith to the *"obeying"* of God's word. As a matter of fact, most of us are just like the Israelites. We confess to believe in the

Lord, to trust the Lord with our whole heart; but often, when it's time to demonstrate our faith, we fail to obey the Lord's commands.

In Numbers we find the Israelites outside the land of Canaan, arguing about whether or not they are able to take the land God told them to go in and spy out. This is the land that God had promised to their forefathers, Abraham, Isaac, and Jacob. As you might recall, the twelve leaders of the tribes of Israel were sent into Canaan, but only two, Joshua and Caleb, came back. When they did, they reported that they could take the land. But the other ten leaders came out shaking in their boots. They declared that they were mere grasshoppers, that the walls were too high, the city was too well fortified, and that going in meant that God had brought them out of Egypt only to have them slaughtered by their enemy in the wilderness.

Now these twelve were leaders had obviously confessed that they trusted the Lord. Yet, only two of them were willing to trust and obey the Lord against all odds. What does it take for us to obey in spite of the odds? Here are three suggestions.

- Never allow your confusion to disrupt your obedience.
- Never be swayed by what you see with your natural eyes.
- Remember that God is able to keep His promises.

A relevant question to raise at this point then is: *Why do those who confess to trust the Lord, end up disobeying the Lord in so many instances?* I have three reasons for such behavior.

Their Faith Was Not As Strong As They Thought

These ten leaders obviously thought they had strong faith in God; but when put to the ultimate test, they failed miserably. They did not trust God to fight for them. They did not trust God to subdue their enemies. They did not trust God to go before them and prepare the way for victory.

They knew that God had promised them the land; but when put to the test, they did not really believe that God was able to deliver on His promise. God had actually instructed them to spy out the land—to look it over. They were swayed by what they saw. They went in on the authority of their God, but they forgot about the power of their God when they saw the giants.

Their faith was not as strong as they thought it was. It's like Peter, when the Lord Jesus Christ told the disciples that He would be taken at the hands of sinful men and crucified, Peter said: *I'll never let them take you! I'll die first; they'll never take you!*

But when his faith was put to the test, we hear Peter denying the Lord—not once, but three times—because he thought his life would also be required if he identified with Jesus. I'm saying that one of the main reasons we don't trust and obey, why we end up disobeying God, is because our faith is not as strong as we thought it was.

You said God was a healer, until you got sick. You said God was deliverer, until our husband succumbed to drugs. You said God was a provider, until you lost your job. You said you trusted God with your very life, until the doctor brought the negative report.

Our faith is often not as we thought it was. While that may be one reason we fail to trust and obey God, there is still another explanation for why we seem to forget that God is the source of our blessings. And it's a biggie.

We Think We Know Better Than God

One of the children of the church where I pastor once said to me: *"Rev. Fuller, if God knows everything, and God knows everything we are going to do before we do it, why does God let people do bad things?"* I told him that God allows people to do bad things because God gives each of us free will. That is, we have the power to choose. We can choose between right and wrong; between good and bad; to obey or to disobey God's will for our lives. That's what happened in the Garden of Eden; Adam and Eve exercised their free will and disobeyed God by eating from the tree of life. They thought they knew better than God. But God allowed them to do it because he created us human beings with minds to think on our own, not as robots that are programmed to do everything the controller of the robot says. Adam and Eve thought they knew better than God and decided that it was okay to eat from the tree of life.

We're like Adam and Eve, aren't we? We think we know more than the God who is known to be omniscient—all knowing; the God who is known to be omnipotent—all powerful; the God who is known to be omnipresent—everywhere at the same time. We think we know more than the God who created the universe and everything in it. We are finite and God in infinite, but we think we know a better way to handle our lives. We are creatures and God is the creator, but we still think we know more than God.

That's why Sarai sent Abram into Hagar when she had not conceived a child after God promised Abram that he would be the father of many nations. They thought they knew more than God. After all, Sarai reasoned, Abram was 90 and she well pass child- bearing age. They tried to wait on God, but God wasn't moving quickly enough, and so Sarai took matters into her own hands. She manipulated the blessing, and gave her young, fertile slave girl, Hagar, to her husband to bear children. Sarai and Abram said they trusted God, but when things got rough, they disobeyed God and took matters into their own hands, trying to fulfill the promise on their own terms.

Have you ever done that? God did not move quickly enough, and so, you took matters into your own hands. You didn't get the job you were praying about, so you took a lower position. You know what kind of mate God intends for you to have, but you got tired of waiting on God; you got tired of trusting God for a mate, and went out and selected one for yourself. Now you've got a mess on your hands.

God said, *be still*, and *I'll make your enemy your footstool.* But you couldn't wait on God. You confront your enemy on your own. That's because we really do think we know more than God knows. We think we know a better way than God knows. We actually think we're smarter than God. So, we end up disobeying God even though we profess faith in Him. A final reason for not trusting and obeying God has to do with doing what we want to do.

We Don't Want What God Wants For Our Lives

The choir sings a song that says, ... *the perfect place for me is in the will of God.* All too often, we want to move around God's will for our lives, don't we? We pray, *Thy will be done!* We sing, *Have thine own way; Lord, have thine own way, Thou art the potter and I am the clay. Make me and mold me after thine will, while I am waiting, yielded and still.* But all too often, we find ourselves singing one thing and living another. Obviously, it's because we don't truly trust God with our whole lives. There are some things that we think we can handle better than God. Some things we know more about than God knows. The bottom line is we do not want what God wants for us.

You may think that I'm being ridiculous; that you've never thought you knew more than God. But think about it; be honest about it. How many times have you willfully disobeyed God because it was just not what you wanted to do? You know what God's word says, but you also know what you want to do. You even know what God spoke in your spirit, but you don't always obey God's directions for your life.

That's what landed Jonah in the belly of a whale. God told him to go to a sinful city called Ninevah, but he did not think the Ninevites were worthy to receive God's word, that they weren't worthy of salvation. Jonah got on a ship headed to Tarshish, in the opposite direction.

Jonah's story, and the story of the Israelites, will let us know that God does not like to be disobeyed. Jonah ended up in the belly of a whale for three long days and nights. The Israelites ended up back in the wilderness for 40 long years, because they refused to trust and to obey God's command. They both understood clearly what God directed them to do, but they thought they knew better than God.

Some people are in a mess because they have not obeyed the word of God for their lives!

They have not followed God's instructions!

They thought they knew a better way!

They just don't agree with God's direction for their lives! They decided to do their own thing!

Well, I want to tell you that what God promised, God is able to deliver!

I want to tell you that it's better to obey God than to order your own steps!

Jesus said, *If you love me, keep my commandments!*

Jesus said, *If you would be my disciple, take up your cross and follow me!*

He didn't have any orientation sessions!

He didn't have a question and answer period,

He said, *If you trust Me, follow Me and obey Me.*

The hymnologist puts it this way:

> *Trust and obey,*
> *For there's no other way,*
> *To be happy in Jesus,*
> *Than to trust and obey.*

That's the message for us today. ***Trust and Obey!***

TRUST AND OBEY
Numbers 14:6-10

STUDY QUESTIONS

1. There is a distinct difference between trusting God and obeying God. Describe a time when you trusted God, but had difficulty in obeying God.

2. What has prevented you from walking in obedience to God?

3. Read Genesis 16. In what ways did Sarai's wavering faith demonstrated a lack of trust in God?

4. In what ways have you tried to manipulate the blessings of God?

5. How have you overcome persecution, rejection, or ridicule by relatives and friends?

6. Using the definitions in this chapter, what are the meanings of trust and faith?

TRUST AND OBEY
Numbers 14:6-10

STUDY QUESTIONS

7. According to the message in this sermon, what do we tend to do when we cannot analyze or figure out a situation?

8. Where in the bible does it say that faith without works is dead?

9. What words did Joshua and Caleb use to warn the Israelites? What did they try to persuade the Israelites to do?

CHAPTER X

WHAT TO DO WHEN YOU GET WEARY IN WELL DOING

Psalm 37:1-9

FRET NOT thyself because of evildoers, neither be thou envious against the workers of iniquity. 2 For they shall soon be cut down like the grass, and wither as the green herb. 3 Trust in the LORD, and do good; so shalt thou dwell in the land, and verily thou shalt be fed. 4 Delight thyself also in the Lord; and he shall give thee the desires of thine heart. 5 Commit thy way unto the LORD; trust also in him; and he shall bring it to pass. 6 And he shall bring forth they righteousness as the light, and thy judgment as the noonday. 7 Rest in the LORD, and wait patiently for him: fret not thyself because of him who prospereth in his way, because of the man who bringeth wicked devices to pass. 8 Cease from anger, and forsake wrath: fret not thyself in any wise to do evil. 9 For evildoers shall be cut off: but those that wait upon the LORD, they shall inherit the earth.

If there is one thing human kind wants, it's justice; to be treated fairly, to get what we think we deserve. One of the many complaints every parent hears down through the years is, "but that's not fair, Mom, you gave Bobby $25.00 and you only gave me $15.00." Or, "John's ice cream cone is bigger than mine, that's not fair!" Just as familiar is the whine, "When Barbara was 16 you let her go on a movie date, why can't I date at 16? It's just not fair!"

Teachers also hear about the quests for justice. "Miss Hines my paper was just as good as his, why did he get an 'A' and I only got a 'B'?" Without a doubt, one of the primary facts of life as we know it, is that people want justice; they want fairness, if not, equality. People don't want to see anyone else get more than they think the person deserves and certainly not to get more than they have. But how many here today have lived long enough to know that life is not always fair. We don't always get what we deserve.

We even go so far as to demand justice from God. We are quick to tell God what we deserve and what we don't deserve. Quick to cry out... why me Lord? Why is my family going through this turmoil? Why did my child turn out like this? Why did my mother have to die? Why did I have to get sick? I'm a good person, why is this happening to me? We're always looking for justice, aren't we?

But I've found out that it's not really justice or fairness we want when it comes to what we deserve from God. When it comes down to our sin debt, we don't want to pay the penalty for our sins. We never ask God to treat us 'justly.' Instead we ask that He show us mercy.

Have you ever noticed that the 37th Psalm is about the need for humankind to have justice, even from God. This Psalm poses the question: *If God loves justice* (verse 28) and *will bring justice to light* (verse 6) then *why are the wicked able to prosper* (verse 7). To put the question from the human side—Why do the righteous suffer?

I can answer that question by sharing with you a passage of scripture that was first quoted to me back in 1976 shortly after I graduated from Boston University. After moving to the Washington, D.C. area to accept a position in my field of Journalism, I soon wondered about fairness when the rug was literally pulled from beneath my feet. There I was, saved, sanctified, filled with the Holy Ghost and jobless. But, I was suddenly out of work because a jealous, envious co-worker plotted to get me released from my new place of employment. Just as unfair was the fact that the person who had hired me, I later discovered, had lied to me about the salary I was suppose to get. I ended up getting much less.

I have to tell you the entire experience left me bitter. And it was then that someone told me to read Psalm 37 and to rest in it. I read and I prayed. I prayed and I rested. Not long afterward, I was invited to join a company that nearly tripled the original salary I had been offered elsewhere. Not only that the new position provided opportunities for travel around the country. And not long after a multitude of doors opened for me, the other business folded; the people who did me wrong were suddenly unemployed. Clearly, sometimes God allows you to see his style of justice. I thank God for Psalm 37; it has taught me many lessons that remain with to this day.

So what should we do when we get weary in well doing? What can you do when you do the right thing, but end up getting the wrong results? What do you do when walk upright and fall on your face. What do you when you live holy but evildoers seem to be prosper while you are out gathering a few sticks to make your last meal and die. It's Psalm 37 that tells us *what to do when we get weary while doing right;* when we get weary in our well doing.

Getting weary means to feel tired of a thing; feeling like giving up; bored; feeling worn out. And I have discovered that often times we find ourselves getting weary when we start looking around and comparing ourselves—our progress—to the progress of others around us. This is particularly so if we think others are getting ahead of us. And if the sanctified truth be told, we see expect to see a contrast between the wicked and the righteous. The righteous expect to prosper, the righteous expect to receive a reward, the righteous expect to advance, and the righteous expect the blessings of God to be bestowed upon them.

But what happens to our spirit when we see the wicked prospering, receiving reward, advancing, being blessed—and we're the ones following the Lord's directions? We don't believe that evildoers ought to expect or receive blessings in their life. They should not be prospering when they are willingly going against everything the Word of God teaches. They in effect, thumb their noses at God and still make more money than you.

Drive Bentleys and never park in the church parking lot. Have stock portfolios and off shore bank accounts and never bring the tithe to the storehouse of the Lord. They sing and dance hard in the smoke filled nightclubs but never make a joyful noise unto the Lord. So how is it that they prosper? How is it that they do so well when we try and follow God's word and sometimes barely make ends meet? In other words: *Why do the wicked prosper and why do the righteous suffer?*

Well, what are we to do when we do the right thing and begin to get weary in well doing. Psalm 37 gives us a roadmap for godliness and for a peace that passeth understanding: *FRET NOT thyself because of evildoers, neither be thou envious against the workers of iniquity.* We're told right from the beginning what the end will be for evildoers. We don't have to wonder. We don't have to plot. We don't have to play pay back. The bible is clear. It tells us in Psalm 37:2 that God will handle things: *For they shall soon be cut down like the grass, and wither as the green herb.* So **Fret Not.**

But know that it takes faith to *fret not* when evildoers seem to be winning. Yet, living by faith and hope has a profound impact on the present, in terms of emotion and behavior. The verb in the do not fret phrase is *hara* and the noun which means wrath—*hema*—have similar root meanings in Hebrew: *To be kindled or to be hot.* And so the Psalmist's advice to *fret not* in verses seven and eight, in today's world means to BE COOL, CHILL OUT! In other words, God is neither blind nor impotent.

God will not be mocked for we are told that, *Whatsoever a person sows, that shall they reap*! Trusting God enables one to live in the present with a certain serenity and peace of heart and mind. But when we get all upset and all out of sorts, when we start fretting, getting upset over that which we have no control, we end up losing cool; we lose our peace of mind. So the first thing to know about what to do, when you get weary in well doing is—Be Cool, *fret not.*

In Psalm 37:3 we are told to *Trust in the LORD* and do *good.* That's good because trusting in the Lord enables you to live constructively in the present and to continue to do good, even when it appears evil pays, quite well. The important thing to remember is that your trust *is in* the Lord, NOT in your enemies. It's when we start trusting our enemies that we're drawn over to the side of evil. But by trusting in the Lord, you are saying that you believe the promises of God; that you know God's word is true concerning you. And that *no weapon formed against you shall prosper* because your God made not only the weapon, but the weapon maker!

Trust in the Lord, and do Good. Don't go "tit for tat" with people. Don't try to do God's job. If you do you'll only get your soul in trouble. *Vengeance is mine,* says the Lord, *I will repay.* God does not need our help taking care of wicked folk. The word says they won't be around long. And in the end you will come out on top and they will wither like the green herb. In other words, things are not always like they seem.

It may look like evil is winning, but we know the end of the story, don't we? It's called *eschatological* hope or future hope. Hope in the promises of God. So when you get weary in well doing—*Trust in the Lord, and do good.* It's important not to forget the *do good* part. For bible says that if your enemy asks for your cloak, give him your coat as well. *Do good* to those who despitefully use you. Everyone knows its easy to treat people good that treat you good. But the bible says we are to *do good,* even to our enemies.

Now we're hearing what's called the *meat* of the Word; the tough parts that don't go down so easily! We want to fret and get all hot headed when we see evil in our midst. But the word tells us to BE COOL and even to do good, while we are waiting on God's promises to be fulfilled.

In verse Psalm 37:4 the Psalmist tells us to *Delight thyself also in the LORD; and he shall give thee the desires of thine heart.* One of the important overall lessons this Psalm teaches us is to keep our eyes and our minds focused on the Lord. That tells us that we are not to give all of our attention to evildoers. We are not to give all our attention to what's wrong with other people who are prospering. Instead, the Word says *delight thyself* in the Lord. In other words, if you keep your mind stayed on Jesus, you will have perfect peace. Delight in the things of God, delight in the goodness of the Lord in your life. Others may be doing better than you, but you're doing okay. Others may have some material things that you want, but the bible tells us to store up treasures in heaven where thieves do not break in and steal.

If you spend more time thinking about the goodness of Jesus, rather than comparing what you have with others, you won't end up fretting. And you will realize that God has already done more than you could ever deserve. *Delight,* enjoy the Lord! Be happy that the Lord saved you. Be happy that your reward is eternal and the wicked person's reward is only temporal. I'm so glad that the verse says that when we delight ourselves in God, He will give us *the desires* of our heart. Now that's good news!

Yet too many of us miss too many of our blessings because we're looking over the fence to see what the Jones' have or envying other people's blessings. But God will give you the godly desires of your own heart when you delight in Him. When it's your pleasure to serve Him. When it's your pleasure to serve his people. When you are just happy to be a part of God's family.

Another way to deal with the wicked is found in verse five of Psalm 37:5 when we are told what to do: *Commit thy way unto the LORD; trust also in him; and he shall bring it to pass.* Committing our way to God means, first, **MEDITATION BEFORE PRAYER.** *Meditation,* says St. Ambrose, " *is the eye wherewith we see God, and prayer is the wing wherewith we flee to Him.* Prayer is not an accidental expression that comes suddenly to the mind; it is the soul's recognition of its own need! And to pray right we must be alone with ourselves, before we are alone with God. Someone has said that when it comes to prayer, *it is better to have a heart without words, than words without a heart.*

Committing our way to God means also that in addition to meditating before prayer, we need a **CONSCIOUSNESS OF**

IGNORANCE. Ignorance at times is humbling. In a previous section of this message I mentioned that *eschatological* or future hope is believing that good is to come to the believer. But even though we want to know all, in reality we know so little. How terrible it would be if we could not commit our way unto the Lord. As one theologian has said, "The heavens are never deaf except when man's heart is dark." In order to commit our way to God then, we need a consciousness of our own ignorance of the things of God. God will handle evildoers when we commit.

Finally, committing our way to God requires CONSCIOUS OBEDIENCE and CHEERFUL ACQUIESCENCE IN HIS WILL. Our dependence on God must end in obedience. Someone once said, *He who prays as he ought will endeavor to live as he prays.* We are never more miserable than when we know the hypocrisy of our own prayers because we are inwardly conscious of our wrong state. We know when we are living without God; we feel sad about it all of the time. When our will is not obedient, we cannot call ourselves followers of the Lamb. We must never forget that that committing our way to God means *conscience obedience* unto God—not merely endurance nor passive submission, but cheerful submission.

It is when our soul comes away from communion with God in the spirit that we see anxiety and worrisome cares leave our hearts. In other words, COMMITTING requires COMMUNION with the LORD! So let's review. Now, what are you going to when you get weary in well doing?

Fret not, Trust the Lord, Delight thyself in Him.

Communion with the Lord.

Now, don't you feel better already? Amen!

WHAT TO DO WHEN YOU GET WEARY IN WELL DOING
Psalm 37:1-9

STUDY QUESTIONS

1. What injustices have you experienced in your Christian walk?

2. What does getting weary symbolize in the Christian walk?

3. What advice would you give someone who is going through a season of weariness because of injustice?

4. When was the last time you grew weary and forgot to FRET NOT? Describe the consequences.

5. What has prevented you in the past year from waiting on the Lord for handling weary situations in your life?

6. How do you manage to BE COOL in the face of seeming injustices in your personal life?

7. Who is the author of Psalm 37?

CHAPTER XI

LORD, HELP ME TO HOLD OUT

Psalm 37:7
*Rest in the LORD, and wait patiently for him; fret not
thyself because of him who prospereth in his way, because of
the man who bringeth wicked devices to pass.*

In Psalm 37, verse seven, David is talking about how the
righteous are to wait on God when it is obvious that the
wicked are advancing and prospering. David tells us to wait
patiently even if it seems the righteous will be left in the dust.

We dealt extensively with this in the last message where
we examined the *roadmap* that David gave us for dealing with
evildoers. First he told us to FRET NOT! Be cool! Take it easy!
Chill out! When it came to the unrighteous, David said don't
worry about them because they won't be around long; they will
soon fade like the grass and wither like the green herb. In verse
three, David tells us explicitly to *Trust in the LORD, and do
good.* Put your trust in the Lord, he said, and not in your
enemies. Know that God has the situation under control and that
God will handle things because God said, *vengeance is mine, I
will repay.*

David advised us to trust God to take care of the wicked
and for us not to get our hands dirty trying to handle God's
business. And in the midst of it all, he stressed that we should *do
good.* Don't try to repay evil, rather do good to those who
spitefully use us. In verse four of Psalm 37 David tells us what
we can do instead: *Delight thyself also in the Lord; and he shall
give thee the desires of thine heart.* Instead of pouting or
complaining or trying to "fix" folk, the Psalmist says we should

115

spend our time delighting in the Lord. Keep your mind on Jesus, David says. Enjoy Jesus! Rest in the fact that God is good and he has promised to give us the desires of our heart. Be happy that our reward is eternal and the wicked person's reward is only temporal.

And besides, David reminds us, we have reason to be happy: we don't have to depend on the wicked to get what we need or want—God is our blessor! God knows how to bless us and when to bless us. So rather than fretting we can delight ourselves in the Lord and watch God bless us all the more. Of course, people are ready to bless the Lord when they've got everything they've prayed for. Most are willing to bless the Lord when they don't have a trouble in the world. But the challenge for the Christian is delighting in the Lord when the enemy seems to be nearby. Delighting in the Lord when we seem to be scraping the bottom of the barrel is tough, especially when the enemy seems to be laughing all the way to the bank. But we have a *roadmap* to keep us on track; to help us keep our eyes on the Lord.

Even though we have been advised to COMMIT TO THE WAY OF THE LORD, some of us have trouble doing this because we have not *lain* before the Lord. Notice that I did not say prayed before the Lord. I'm talking about Meditation, being still. Over the years I've learned that MEDITATION MUST COME BEFORE PRAYER, if we are to commit or be in communion with the Lord. We have already learned that St. Ambrose summed this up when he said that "Meditation is the eye wherewith we see God, and prayer is the wing wherewith we flee to Him.

As I pointed out in the last message, prayer is not an accidental expression that comes suddenly to the mind. It is, rather, meditation that leads to prayer. Prayer comes as a result of the soul recognizing its need. And in order to pray effectively, we must go inward. We must, in other words, be alone with ourselves, before we can be alone with God. While prayer meetings are great and wonderful, you had better have a *prayer closet* at home.

It amazes me that I still hear folk say that they don't know how to pray, or they don't know what to say. But I'm here to say that you may think you don't know how to pray, you may not even remember the last time you prayed, but there will come a time when trouble will remind you *how* to pray! Just get sick enough, and you won't care about the correct words, the correct formula, or the correct posture—you'll cry out to the Lord like you've been praying every day. I'm reminded that when prayer was all Hidalgo had left, he called upon his god.

To summarize then, David has given us in Psalm 37, four steps for dealing with evildoers without fretting ourselves into bad health.

1. FRET NOT
2. TRUST IN THE LORD, AND DO GOOD
3. DELIGHT IN THE LORD
4. COMMIT TO THE WAY OF THE LORD

And after all is said and done in the above verses, David tells us what to do next in verse seven when he says *Rest in the LORD, and wait patiently for him.* But if after all the wisdom imparted by David, we are to be still before the Lord and wait patiently we may need to scream out: LORD, HELP ME TO HOLD ON!

Have you ever prayed and prayed, waited and waited, and still have no evidence of an answer? Have you ever been frustrated over not seeing any movement or progress when it comes to your prayers? Are you at the point of giving up? Are you ready to throw in the towel and say later for the whole thing? Then, perhaps, you have not waited in the right way! Listen, waiting in the *wrong way* removes you from the *right place*—the place where the Lord can meet you.

David, gives us instructions on WAITING in Psalm 37. We learn from him that there is a right way—a fruitful way—and a wrong way—an unfruitful way. And if you are not waiting in the right way, then you are not in the right place. You're not, in other words, in the place where the Lord can meet you and bless you.

Now notice that the Psalmist does not *merely* say wait. David tells us to BE STILL and wait. Cool your heels and wait. And notice he just doesn't say wait. He tells us how to wait— PATIENTLY. So I'm here to remind you in this message that too often we block our own blessings because we have not learned, as Christians, how to wait, HOW TO HOLD OUT until change comes. Just as Jesus' disciples asked him to teach them how to pray, we need to ask him to teach us HOW TO WAIT. Each of us need to pray, Lord, teach me how to wait; Lord, help me to hold out!

Waiting is by no means an easy art to perfect. I believe that waiting is so difficult for most of us, at least for me, because it means that we have no control over the matter. We simply have to wait for God to move in our lives. And God only moves in God's time, not our time. If we're honest, waiting is something we do when we can't do anything else. It's not usually our first choice of things to do. We wait usually because we have exhausted all of the avenues we know. We wait because we've tried everything else and failed. We wait because we finally realize that God is waiting for us to take our hands off the problem and put the problem in God's hand. We end up having to learn to let God handle things.

Not too many of us like to wait on God. And if the truth is told, we just don't know how to wait, anyway, in the right way. When I say that we are not in the right place when we are not waiting in the right way, I am not talking about a physical place, but a spiritual place. So my purpose here is to give some instruction on how to make the best of our seasons of waiting on the Lord. I want to encourage you to not give up, but to *learn* to wait on the Lord. And for anyone who says, *but I've been waiting so long*, I want to show you how to HOLD ON. I want to share with you about constructive waiting, *purposeful waiting,* productive waiting, or waiting the bible prescribed way. Here's how to HOLD OUT!

The first thing to do in this waiting process is to *be still* to *be quiet*. In other words, calm down, settle down! I dare say that many of you are doing the wrong things while you call yourself waiting on God. And that's why you are not getting answers from God. We say we are waiting when really we are still trying to work things out, still trying to handle the situation ourselves, still trying to change the person, still trying to open the door, still trying to close the door, still trying to find the right husband/wife, still trying to change our bad habits, or still trying to fix what's wrong in your children's lives.

The problem is clearly that *we're* trying, working, and battling instead of *being still* before the Lord; being quiet before the Lord. We're not, in other words, open before the Lord. Yet, we will only see results when you and I learn to *be still* before the Lord! The Lord is probably sitting back watching and saying, "When you take your hands off the matter, then I'll handle it. But I refuse to arm wrestle the problem from you. But give it to me and I'll bear it." *Come unto me all ye that weary and heavy laden and I will give you rest. Take my yoke upon you and learn of me, for my yoke is easy and my burden is light.*

God is saying that we can cast all of our cares upon Him, for He cares for us. Yet, the hardest thing for most of us to do is to be still and wait patiently; clear signs that we haven't learned to totally trust God. That means we're also not praying the right way. We do *pray and tell*. We tell God what God should do! We tell Him how to do it and even when He should do it. We're in effect saying, *Do it right now, God.* But the most effective prayer we can pray when trouble finds our address is: *Speak Lord, for your servant is listening.*

Prayers that only tell God what to do, leave no room for God to speak to our hearts about what our needs. When we do all the talking during prayer, we fail to leave room for God's voice. We can't hear what he is telling us to do or not to do. But God wants us to spend some time *being still* before Him so that He can minister to us.

Mediations must come before prayer. We cannot commit to the Lord's way until we still our minds, still our wandering thoughts, still our troubled hearts, and calm our fears, *before* we begin to pray. We've heard the same message in a song that says: "If you want to know God's plan for your life, get in the spirit, let the Lord minister to you!

Holding out is all about being still before the Lord, quieting our thoughts, calming our racing minds, and holding our fiery, negative tongues. I'm talking about being still mentally and spiritually. This does not necessarily mean sitting or laying down. Being still is not so much about posture, as it is about our inner being. And what happens when we are still; when we are in a posture of waiting? David tells us in verses one through three in Psalm 40 when he said: *I waited patiently for the Lord and he inclined unto me and heard my cry. He brought me up also out of a horrible pit, out of the miry clay, and set my feet upon a rock, and established my goings. And he hath put a new song in my mouth, even praise unto our God; many shall see it, and fear, and shall trust in the Lord.*

When we are busy trying to handle everything ourselves, play God, or do things our way, we miss out on blessings. Oh, if we just sit down a minute and quiet our spirits, God will show us who He really is. God will show you and me that he can handle our enemies. God will show He can solve our problems. God will show you that He has everything you need and he's willing to give you what you need. And so when we pray—Lord, help me to Hold Out, what we are really saying is Lord, help me to TRUST you! Lord, help me to wait on you. Lord, help me to wait on you. Lord, help me to know that you know exactly what I need. Lord, help me to sit back and leave the driving to you. Lord, help me to hold out, to be still—until my change comes.

And I see the reward for those who wait over in Isaiah, the Book of the Prophet. When you get weary in well doing, ready Chapter 40. Read it when you think your waiting is in vain. Read it when you don't think the Lord is not moving fast enough for you.

> *Hast thou not known? Hast thou not heard, that the everlasting God, the LORD, the Creator of the ends of the earth, fainteth not, neither is weary? There is no searching of his understanding. 29 He giveth power to the faint; and to them that have no might he increaseth strength. 30 Even the youths shall faint and be weary, and the young men shall utterly fall: 31 But they that wait upon the LORD shall renew their strength; they shall mount up with wings as eagles; they shall run, and not be weary; and they shall walk, and not faint.*
>
> —Isaiah 40:28-31

God is still in charge, so just keep on praying: LORD, help me to hold on!

LORD, HELP ME TO HOLD OUT!

LORD, HELP ME TO HOLD OUT
Psalm 37:7

STUDY QUESTIONS

1. In what direction do you move when you get weary in well doing? Toward God? Away from God?

2. The Psalmist, David, provides four suggestions in the 37TH Psalm for dealing with evildoers. What are they and in what verses are they found?

3. What has prevented you in the past three months from holding out and waiting patiently on the Lord?

4. Compare the advice of David, the Psalmist, and Isaiah, the Prophet for not becoming weary?

5. What is the reward promised in Isaiah 40:28-31 for those who wait on the Lord?

CHAPTER XII

LAUNCH OUT

St. Luke 5:1-11

And it came to pass, that as the people pressed upon him to hear the word of God, he stood by the lake of Gennesaret. 2 And saw two ships standing by the lake: but the fishermen were gone out of them, and were washing their nets. 3 And he entered into one of the ships, which was Simon's, and prayed him that he would thrust out a little from the land. And he sat down, and taught the people out of the ship. 4 Now when he had left speaking, he said unto Simon, *Launch out into the deep, and let down your nets for a draught.* 5 And Simon answering said unto him, Master, we have toiled all the night, and have taken nothing: nevertheless at thy word I will let down the net. 6 And when they had this done, they inclosed a great multitude of fishes: and their net brake. 7 And they beckoned unto their partners, which were in the other ship, that they should come and help them. And they came, and filled both the ships, so that they began to sink. 8 When Simon Peter saw it, he fell down at Jesus' knees, saying, Depart from me; for I am a sinful man, O Lord. 9 For he was astonished and all that were with him, at the draught of the fishes which they had taken: 10 And so was also James, and John the sons of Zebedee, which were partners with Simon, *Fear not; from henceforth thou shall catch men.* 11 And when they had brought their ships to land, they forsook all, and followed him.

Desperate people don't *launch out* unless they have faith; unless they are able to commit to the way of God. As Jesus explained to Simon Peter in St. Luke 5:4, the words *launch out,* mean for one to move from where they are to a place of greater depth. But you should know that when you *launch out* into the deep things of God, you're aren't always going to be able to see exactly where it is you are going. For once you leave safe, shallow waters, you probably won't be able to see the bottom.

Oh, it takes faith to move out from the comfort of shore to places where you can't predict the outcome. It takes faith to push back from what you know and head for a place where only God can keep you. Stepping out on faith takes faith, doesn't it!

In order for Peter to obey Jesus' instructions to launch out, he had to move on *blind obedience*. Jesus has just finished speaking to the crowds when he told Peter, *Launch out into the deep, and let down your nets for a draught*. Now it's easy to be obedient when what the person is saying makes sense to you. But Simon Peter was being asked to catch fish where he knew none existed. Having worked all night without catching anything, Simon had good reason not to be obedient because he had been there, done that, and still *no* fish. You could almost hear him thinking to himself—*Didn't you see us wash our nets, Master? Didn't you see us go out and come back with nothing?*

Well, let the incident in St. Luke be a good reminder that God does not move *at our convenience*. Look at how Jesus showed up and took over in a very unassuming manner and at a most inopportune time. Never-the-mind that the men had worked all night at catching fish. Jesus came when he was ready!

Sometimes when we are at our wit's end, when we are at the end of our collective ropes, that's when we are right at the beginning of blessings. So don't faint when hard times hit, pray! Pray to hold on and hold out. Don't let the night beat you. Trust and obey. For none of us are exempt from hardships and heartaches or setbacks and tribulations. There's plenty of evidence in the Scripture that when your back is against the wall, it's time to *Launch Out*. It's time to trust and obey!

Launching out requires the kind of obedience that must come before true worship can happen. If we have not done what God told us to do, how can we truly worship. Instead, we'll find ourselves looking around and thinking that people have lost their minds. But it is because people have obeyed before attempting to worship that they can be free in worship. Obedient people can give God true praise. In fact, if you want to know why some church folk seem so mean and unhappy or act ugly or always complaining, it's because they have not obeyed. And disobedience will leave you miserable—even in the sanctuary.

My husband found that out at the beginning of the new year when he said God told him to give more money than he had planned to give. He had not received a salary increase. He had not been out to preach. But he said the Lord told him to give more anyway. I learned that my husband, the *Rev. Dr. Stanley Fuller* tried to make a bargain with the Lord by saying he would give more after he paid off our Christmas bills and the college tuition fees. But when he tried to go into the pulpit, he said he heard the Lord say again, *"Give more."* That time, he turned immediately around and acted like an obedient servant. He left the sanctuary and went back to his office where he wrote another check! Now that's obedience. That *blind obedience* resulted in his having what he described as a wonderful worship service. And when you think about it, simple disobedience is probably the main reason so many churches are dying on the vine.

A reading of St. Luke also shows us that the difference between great success and great failure is JESUS! Here we had the same nets, same boat, same lake. Without Jesus, the men came back empty handed. The next time they went out and got something, Jesus was in the boat. Obedience brought success!

If you think Jesus is not watching out for you recall that Jesus saw two ships standing by the lake. But this was a fishing town. Every family made their living fishing in the lake. At any given time there were at least 20,000 fishing boats, yet Jesus somehow only saw two of them. And among all the fishermen out that day, isn't it something that Jesus joined Peter, James, and John. Know this: Jesus knows how to find you in the midst of a sea of other people.

Now some may call it a Holy coincidence when Jesus shows up. Thank God that he found you and me. How did you meet him? It may have been a preached word or a video. Maybe you ran into someone at the mall and they invited you to church. BAM! Jesus showed up in your life. Holy Coincidence.

But all too often we don't succeed because we refuse to take God at God's Word. We don't believe what God says. Some of us are too educated; too learned... to simply move by faith. God says *launch out*—don't tell me about your expertise or credentials, I already know you; you apparently don't know me!

We've blown our blessings because God said *launch out* but we stayed in our places of seemingly safety. But no matter what the situation looks like, the safest time for the Christian to move is when God says **Launch Out**.

We would do well to remember those who came before us who walked in faith. They are the ones who launched out into the deep and built the Wilberforce and Hampton Universities, Barber-Scotia, Shaw University, St. Augustine, and countless other historically Black colleges. Those who walked in faith launched out without Ph.D.'s or even undergraduate degrees or high school diplomas. They had no six-figure salaries. With almost nothing, these faith workers built what we can't even seem to maintain today—faith. They had faith in a God who can do anything but fail.

We need to be ready to launch out on faith because God's timing is not our timing. Like Peter, we need to learn to say, *At your word!* Launching out into the deep means you will not be able to see the end of the matter. Deep means deep! If you can't see the bottom and you can't see the outcome, then what's required is stepping out and deeply by faith.

I have come to understand that too many people are more interested in Religion than they are in Relationship with Jesus. They hold fast to religious traditions. Some men and women go so far as to say they can't sit under a woman pastor. I ran across a note in the back of my bible recently that read: Religion is for folk who are afraid of going to hell. But Relationship is for people who have already been to Hell! I see a clue for someone. Launch out. Stop standing on religious traditions and focus on developing a Relationship with Jesus. Don't we know by now that if we keep doing the same thing the same way, we'll just get the same thing we've always gotten! It's time for the Saints of God to take Jesus at his word and LAUNCH OUT!

The scripture before us makes that point. If you read it carefully you will see that Jesus challenges Peter, James, and John, his newly called disciples, in at least three areas:

1. **Obedience**
2. **Faith**
3. **Submission to His will.**

And let me say right now that the three actually go hand in hand. One does not work without the other: obedience leads to greater faith, greater faith leads to greater submission, and it takes all three to seriously LAUNCH OUT.

Well, Rev. Ann, you might say, *what's this Launch Out thing you're talking about?* The Bible says that Jesus stands at the door and knocks. If any person opens the door, he will come in and sup with you. He will come in and have fellowship with you because Jesus desires relationship—not religious practices that leave you in the same Hell you've been in all along! Do you know that you could have stayed at home and caught Hell or stayed in your same old life style and caught Hell? But remember that throughout his ministry, Jesus had to struggle with religious leaders who would not recognize that Jesus was the fulfillment of the Law. That his agenda was not to become mired in their traditions and practices that had not worked and could not work. He came to die for the sins of the world, to set the captives free, and to preach deliverance to those who were bound.

If any person is in Christ he is a new creation, old things are passed away, behold all things are become new! The correct interpretation is that all things are becoming new—day by day, little by little. How many know that this Christian Life is a journey? We don't complete the journey in one day. Jesus entered Peter's boat and first gave him simple instructions that he could handle before telling him to launch out into the deep. Tell somebody—Let Jesus IN!

Now remember that what we're hearing in St. Luke is the story of how Jesus called the first disciples. How many of you remember how difficult it was for you to let Jesus into your heart; to allow Jesus into your personal space. Could you let someone else take control of your life? Simon must have been tired. But when Jesus knocked, he opened the door and let him on board. Listen, I believe that since Simon Peter was there, he must have been listening to what Jesus had said to the crowds. And the message must have touched him because his second act of blind obedience came right after Jesus finished speaking to the crowds.

When told to launch out, Simon simply said, *If you say so, I will let down the net.* Simon Peter was a fast learner. He must have felt the power of God on his boat. He must have known that this was no ordinary man telling him to Launch Out into the Deep. So he said, *at thy word I will let down the net.* Peter and everyone around saw for themselves that obedience pays off. The bible says the men caught so many fish that their nets were beginning to break and they had to signal for a second boat to come out and help carry the fish back. But both boats were so full they also were about to break. Aw, the lesson for us in this message is that obedience brings overflow blessings.

Oh, you can do the ordinary on your own. You can just get by on your own. You may be able to make ends meet on your own. But when you get ready to receive overflow, when you get in position for greater rewards, and when you learn to expect more—it's going to take blind obedience to Jesus. When Jesus says LAUNCH OUT, just do it! No matter how illogical it sounds—do it!

Do you know that Jesus does not give you overflow or more, just for personal gain or your personal comfort and use? But overflow blessings are for Kingdom Building. Overflow blessings are for everyone to see the power of God in your life and your ministry. It's just NOT about you; it's not about your pastor. The overflow our church is experiencing is for the larger community so it too can see the Power of God! Through overflow, God is gathering fishers of men because we will never follow until we see His power at work. And it worked! These skilled fishermen dropped their nets, left their boats, and followed Jesus to do greater works in his name. Jesus taught them to become his disciples/fishers of men and women!

I don't know about you, but that's the kind of obedience I want. Obedience that responds: *If you say so Lord, I'll do it.* Anybody can sit on the comfortable, safe shoreline and wish or grumble and complain—but it takes faith to say:

> *Lord, if you say so I'll launch out to places I've never been before.*
> *Lord if you say so, I'll step out on nothing and expect everything.*
> *Lord, if you say so, I'll preach in season and out of season.*

Lord if you say so, we'll feed the hungry even though we're unemployed; we'll clothe the naked even though our children don't have all they need; we'll house the homeless even though we don't have money to pay our own mortgage.

Lord, if you say so, I'll go where you tell me to go and do what you tell me to do—no matter what it looks like; no matter what others say, no matter if I've tried before and failed. Even if your way is not the conventional way, even if every one thinks I've lost my mind, Lord, if you say so, I'll keep on telling sinners of your salvation plan.

I'll keep hope alive in your people!

I'll stand on the wall and cry loud and spare not.

I'll tell the lost that they can be saved. I'll tell the hopeless that there is hope. I'll tell the nation that when the Lord says *Launch out into the deep*, it will take more than one boat to haul in the catch!

LAUNCH OUT! LAUNCH OUT!

LAUNCH OUT
St. Luke 5:1-11

STUDY QUESTIONS

1. Where do you go for your spiritual fishing? Shallow waters or deep waters?

2. What risk did the men take by launching out into deep waters? What risk have you taken when you launched out into deeper waters?

3. In what ways can religious traditions or beliefs about roles and relationships keep people from launching out?

4. Describe a "deep water" excursion at the commanding of Jesus in your life?

5. What are the three ways in which the First Disciples were tested?

6. What prevents some desperate people from taking God at his word?

CHAPTER XIII

IF YOU SAY SO

St. Luke 5:1-11

And it came to pass, that as the people pressed upon him to hear the word of God, he stood by the lake of Gennesaret. 2 And saw two ships standing by the lake: but the fishermen were gone out of them, and were washing their nets.

In the last chapter we reflected on launching out into deep waters as Jesus told Simon Peter to do in St. Luke 5:1-11. I said that Jesus went onto Simon Peter's fishing boat for the primary reason of challenging Simon Peter's faith, his Obedience and his willingness to submit. We learned that if Jesus is going to change our lives so that He can use us, we must first allow Jesus into our lives, our hearts – our space, if you will.

We said that *Jesus stands at the door and knocks and if we open the door, he will come in and sup with us* and once he develops relationship with us, he begins to change our lives for the better. And so Jesus was teaching by the lake of Gennesaret, other versions call it the Lake Galilee, and others the Sea of Galilee. A great crowd had gathered to hear Jesus' words and the press was so great that Jesus got onto Simon Peter's boat and told him to 'push off a little from the land.' Then Jesus sat down and continued teaching the people. The bible said that when Jesus finished his teaching, he said to Simon *Put out into the deep water and let down your nets for a catch.*

You'll remember that Simon Peter protested saying that they had just returned from fishing all night and caught nothing. Peter must have reasoned to himself: *Why in the world would they want to go back and fail some more.* They were skilled

131

fishermen and if they did not catch anything, there must have been a reason. And we surmised that although it was the same boat, the same nets and the same lake, Peter was right to obey because the difference that time was that Jesus was on the boat! And that makes all the difference in the world. How many of us know the number of times we made a mess of our lives, our careers, our homes, our jobs—before Jesus came aboard. And not much has changed, except for the fact that now we know Jesus rules and reigns in our lives, and everything is different!

But different only if you too become able to say, *IF YOU SAY SO* just like Peter. In fact, I want to suggest that all too often we don't succeed in life simply because *we refuse* to take God at God's word. We simply do not believe what God says. Not really. We're like Peter and the other fishermen, we think *we* know better than Jesus. We think our station in life, or our educational achievements make us smarter than Jesus. We think that because we've been around the block a few times we know how to handle our lives better than Jesus does. But Simon Peter, who was about to become a disciple of Jesus, taught us an important lesson for our Christian Journey.

Learn from Simon Peter's encounter and know that the Lord comes to examine our Faith, not our credentials or our ability to reason. But faith, is what counts with the Lord. As you may recall when Jesus came onto Peter's boat, just like when he comes into our lives, He comes to challenge our *faith, obedience and submission*. And trust me, it took all three of these elements for Peter to respond the way he did—to launch out into the deep waters and put down his nets for a catch! You can be sure that his personal instincts told him otherwise. Peter had fished those same waters for a lifetime—he knew the habits of the fish in Lake Genneseret. But it was faith that caused Peter to say, *If you say so*, to Jesus. In other words he was saying *at your word I'll do what seems impossible, even the ridiculous—but only at your Word, Lord.* He obeyed and he submitted to the power of the Almighty. That's faith! And understand that it is the kind of faith that it takes to launch out into the deep things of God. Faith that simply takes God at God's word, no matter what it looks like. Faith that says "Lord, I don't know how to swim in deep water, but I believe that you are my life jacket. Faith that says 'Lord, you know all things!' So, *if you say so!*

There is a story in St. Luke 7:1-10 that further illustrates my point this morning about the importance of having solid faith in God. About how much the Lord Jesus values our simple yet solid faith in Him. The story is of Jesus healing the Centurion soldier's servant. Jesus had just finished teaching the people and the bible says he entered Capernaum. There, a Centurion Soldier had a servant whom he valued highly, and who was ill and close to death. When he heard about Jesus, he sent some Jewish elders to him, asking him to come and heal his servant.

When they came to Jesus, they appealed to him earnestly, saying, He is worthy of having you do this for him, for he loves our people, and it is he who built our synagogue for us. And Jesus went with them, but when he was not far from the house, the Centurion sent friends to say to him *"Lord, do not trouble yourself, for I am not worthy to have you come under my roof. Therefore I did not presume to come to you. But only speak the word, and let my servant be healed.* Speak the Word! Now that's faith!

That's the kind of faith that moves the very heart of Jesus! And not only does the man have mountain moving faith, but this foreigner has a deep reverence for the Lord. Jesus must have been a bit taken aback. He traveled here at the man's request and the Jews recommendation, and now the man says I don't want you to come either into my presence or into my home—not out of disrespect, but out of sheer reverence. He sends word by his friends that he is not worthy to be in the presence of the Lord; that's why he did not personally bring his request. And when Jesus heard this he was amazed at him, and turning to the crowd that followed him he said, *I tell you, this is the greatest faith I have found anywhere, even in Israel. And* the bible said that those who had been sent to Jesus went back to the house where they found the servant in good health. Somebody say 'speak the word!'

Listen church, he said *even in Israel.* Think about that. Among all the so-called 'religious folk,' all the priests and rulers in the synagogue, I have not found such faith! Among those who claim to know the Letter of the Law, pray three times a day, look down on folk who are not just like them—in all of Israel, there was not such faith! What kind of faith is that? Faith that will take God at His word. Faith that will step out on nothing and expect everything. Faith that says, *just speak your word Lord, and my servant will be healed.* And look at the character of the centurion soldier Jesus.

He had never laid eyes on Jesus to my knowledge. He had only heard of his power and had a deep reverence for him! This man is a leader, a ruler himself. He says in St. Luck 5:8, *"for I also am a man under authority, with soldiers under me; and I say to one, 'go,' and he goes, and to another, 'come,' and he comes, and to my slave, 'do this,' and the slave does it.* And remember the centurion soldier came highly recommended by Jesus' own people. They said, *Jesus, he is worthy of your coming because he has loved your people and he built a synagogue for us.*

Yet here is a foreigner who senses the divinity of Jesus and does not even feel worthy to be in the same room with Jesus. He simply spoke his faith: You don't need to come here and see him or lay hands on him, just speak your Word—and I know my servant will be healed. Who is praying for you like that today!

That man's FAITH made a major impression on Jesus. Some think Jesus should be impressed by our titles, by our positions of authority, by our achievements, or by our wealth and educational accomplishments. You know like I do that titles and position and wealth can pass away. But, Praise the Lord, faith will stand the test of time. Let's say that again—FAITH WILL STAND THE TEST OF TIME! If truth be told, if we had the Centurion Soldier's credentials, some of us would have been insulted had Jesus *not entered* our homes. But when Jesus heard of the man's faith he told the crowd—*I tell you, I have not seen such faith in all of Israel—in all of the so called 'holy' people of God!*

This foreigner demonstrated the same kind of faith as Peter. Jesus said, *Put out into the deep water and let down your nets for a catch.* After Peter mentioned that he and the other men had worked all night without catching anything, he quickly said, *Yet if you say so, I will let down the nets.* And I just want the heavenly record to show that that's the kind of faith and obedience I want the Lord to see in my personal life. A kind of 'send your word' faith; a kind of *if you say so* faith! I want faith to be able to launch out when the Lord says so, no matter what it looks like; to be able to trust the Lord's word in any and every situation. To know that if the Lord said it, I can take it to the bank. If the Lord says so, I don't have to understand it or be in control, I can take Him at his Word. Yes! God said it, I believe it, and that settles it for me!

And I hear the Lord telling my church to *Launch Out on his Word.* To stretch out on his promises. To rest in his revelations. To write the vision and make it plain that those that read it shall run with it. Aw, I hear the Lord saying it's time for the Church to Launch out from it's comfort zone and do the work of evangelism. Do the work of Missions. Do the work of building community—even in the midst of economic hard times. Lord, Baltimore City is threatening to lay-off thousands more school teachers, but send your Word, Lord and Mt. Calvary will open her own school and employ your people.

Just send your Word! Send your Word, Lord and I'll lead our church into becoming the HUB of this community. We won't be just Mt. Calvary A.M.E. Church in Towson, Maryland, we'll be *Greater* Mt. Calvary A.M.E. Village! Worship Center! Education Center! Family Life Center! Recreational Center! Whatever your people need... Just send your Word, Lord and we'll feed the hungry, even though we're unemployed; we'll clothe the naked, even though our children don't have all they need. We'll build houses for the homeless, even though we don't have money to pay our own mortgages. Lord, just send your word! Let the record show: I want faith to go where you tell me to go, do what you tell me to do, say what you tell me to say…no matter what 'they say.' I want to do what *you* say! It won't matter if I've tried before and failed! It won't matter if people think I've lost my mind. Enough of them already think I'm crazy for having my congregation pay off a million dollar mortgage in five years. In the midst of a near depression, we did it! We held a mortgage burning ceremony after only five years because you said, *It is So*, and you backed us up! So, yes, keep on sending your Word and I'll keep on telling sinners of your salvation plan.

Keep on sending those broken in spirit and I'll keep telling your people that there is hope for the hopeless. I'll stand on the wall and cry loud and spare not. I'll tell the LOST they can still be saved. I'll tell the SICK there is a balm in Gilead. I'll tell the PRISONERS that you came to set the captives free. Oh yes, and I'll tell nations about your mighty power to take ordinary people and do *extraordinary* things! Yes, Lord, I'll even leave my comfort zones to FOLLOW YOU!!! Lord, *if you say so!* Just send your word and I'll follow. At your word I'll step out on nothing and expect everything.

I don't want to be like the rich young ruler who asked Jesus: *What must I do to inherit eternal life?* But when Jesus gave him the answer and said, *Sell all you have and follow me*, the young man went away sorrowful. I don't want to be like Naaman who went to the Prophet in Samaria. He was disappointed because even though the Prophet did not come out and greet him, he told Naaman to go dip his leprous body in the Jordon river seven times. Naaman did not receive the Prophet's word well; he even became indignant. By doing so Naaman almost missed his healing!!! He's a good example of why we need to be able to say, *At your word Lord!*

We need to be able to say: *Just send your word!* Now that's a faith that will not shrink even if pressed by every foe. I know because I left a wonderful job at the Baltimore Convention Center at your Word! I know because I was assigned to be the pastor at a little church in Cecilton, Maryland after I gave up my good paying job.

At your word, I later left Cecilton to become the first female preacher at historic Mt. Calvary African Methodist Episcopal Church on the backside of East Towson.

At your Word, I'm a WITNESS! I know without a doubt that when you and I launch out into deeper waters God will be there. Say it with me...

If you say so, Lord!

Launch OUT! Expect more in 2004 and any other year. Launch out... on His Word! Be a worthy servant who does not hesitate to say—IF YOU SAY SO, LORD!

IF YOU SAY SO
St. Luke 5:1-11

STUDY QUESTIONS

1. How did the Centurion soldier's faith compare to the disciples' faith when Jesus said, Launch out into the deep?

2. How did the Centurion soldier get such faith? Who told the foreigner about Jesus' power to heal?

3. Why did the Centurion soldier not want Jesus to come to his home?

4. In what way would you feel comfortable or uncomfortable for Jesus to come into your home?

5. How were the disciples rewarded for their faith? How was the Centurion soldier reward?

6. When was the last time you were directed to launch out?

CHAPTER XIV

WHEN GOD IS THE CAUSE OF YOUR DESPERATION

St. Luke 1:26-33

And in the sixth month the angel Gabriel was sent from God unto a city of Galilee, named Nazareth, 27 To a virgin espoused to a man whose name was Joseph, of the house of David; and the virgin's name was Mary. 28 And the angel came in unto her and said, Hail, thou that art highly favored, the Lord is with thee: blessed art thou among women. 29 And when she saw him, she was troubled at his saying, and cast in her mind what manner of salutation this should be. 30 And the angel said unto her, Fear not, Mary: for thou hast found favour with God. 31 And, behold, thou shalt conceive in thy wound, and bring forth a son, and shalt call his name JESUS. 32 He shall be great, and shall be called the Son of the Highest: and the Lord God shall give unto him the throne of his father David: 33 And he shall reign over the house of Jacob for ever; and of his kingdom there shall be no end.

The *New Webster's Dictionary* describes a vessel as a hollow utensil for holding liquids or solids, a ship, or a person. But it's not just a dictionary that calls us *vessels*, the Word of God does also—some of honor and some of dishonor.

In Acts 9:15 the Lord tells Ananias to go and find Saul of Tarsus on a street called Straight. He says, *Go thy way: for he is a chosen VESSEL unto me, to bear my name before the Gentiles, and kings and the children of Israel...* Ananias knew Saul to be a slayer of those in the Way, that is, of Christians. Paul writes in 2 Timothy 2:21, 22 that, *If a man therefore purge himself from these, he shall be a vessel unto honour, sanctified, and meet for the master's use, and prepared unto every good work. Flee also youthful lusts, but follow righteousness, faith, charity, peace, with them that call on the Lord out of a pure heart.*

Then, in 2 Corinthians 4:7 we are told, *But we have this treasure in earthen vessels, that the excellency of the power may be God, and not of us.* In other words, we won't be getting any big heads when God uses us to do extraordinary things. Because it is not unusual for some chosen vessels to resist being used by a God that does extraordinary things, I want to talk in this message about those times **WHEN GOD IS THE CAUSE OF YOUR DESPERATION.**

Read all of St. Luke 1 and you will quickly see that Mary is God's *chosen vessel.* But I wish to submit that Mary was chosen first of all out of need. God needed a vessel, not a jar or a ship, but *someone* to deposit a divine assignment into. And my intention is to show you why I believe God chose Mary, the virgin girl from Nazareth, for a divine assignment.

The evidence? First, God found Mary to be a *Willing Vessel.* Ever notice how you get desperate when you're not willing to do the right thing? Well, in St. Luke when the angel revealed God's plan for Mary to become the mother of the Son of God she did not understand it at all, especially since she was a virgin. But her immediate response was not "Why?" but as St. Luke 1:38 shows she said, *I am the Lord's Servant, be it unto me according to your word.'* That's the language of a *Willing Vessel.* This young girl Mary who was waiting to be married to Joseph, the man of her dreams, was willing to set her own plans aside to be of use to the Lord.

The bible says, Mary was espoused to Joseph. And so according to the Law, they were married... but the marriage had not been consummated. They had plans, yet Mary was willing to set them aside. Her wedding date was set, the reception hall rented, the honeymoon planed, yet just as Mary was about to become Joseph's bride she told the angels, *I am the Lord's servant, be it unto me according to thy word.* Now I have performed hundreds of weddings in the sanctuary of several churches so I couldn't but think what the brides would have done had their wedding been abruptly called off, even by God. You know, brides fall apart at the drop of a hat. They have the pre-wedding jitters. Everything is a potential problem—she gained five pounds after the seamstress finished her wedding dress, the bridesmaids dress turned out to be the wrong shade of pink, the shoes weren't died the right color, or she breaks a nail.

Out of desperation some brides even begin worrying about whether the groom will even show up. Yes, most brides get the wedding jitters. But Mary, the bride-to-be, rose to the occasion for the Lord. So it appears to me that God chose this vessel named Mary because He knew that Mary was willing to *decrease* so God could *increase*. She was willing to trust God even when her life was fully interrupted and she did not understand. She was willing even though she did not know God's plan or His purpose for her life. She had had her own plans; plans that did not include bearing anyone's son other than Joseph's.

But because the virgin Mary was willing to be obedient and follow God's plan she did not know the desperation that God caused. She was willing to give her life over to God's purpose. And get this, out of all the virgins in the land, Mary was chosen by God *because* Mary was a *Willing Vessel*. What blessings are we missing out on because we are not willing vessels?

But there's another reason I believe God chose Mary over other virgins in the land. Mary was not only a *Willing Vessel*, but she was a *Waiting Vessel*. That is to say, Mary was chosen by God because she knew how to Wait. Too many brides and grooms jump the broom too fast these days. By the time the wedding day comes, there's not much new to experience. The marriage bed is old hat, the couple has already been together and been on all kinds of trips together. Many have lived together and started families together. It seems that no one wants to wait anymore, doesn't it? But not Mary! Mary knew how to wait for sex after marriage, according to God's law.

Listen, a *waiting vessel* is not so full of itself that God's will cannot be done in his or her life. Mary was chosen because she was not so full of what she wanted. She was not so preoccupied with what she desired that she placed her own flesh above what God desired for her. Mary knew how to WAIT!

By the way, it also came to me that this was not Mary's first encounter with the Holy Spirit. It came to me that Mary must have had a solid relationship with the Lord prior to the angel's appearance. She just didn't walk into a relationship with God because an angel spoke to her. Mary obviously knew something about God; she must have had a relationship already in place. You see, in order to set her plans for her wedding aside, she must have had a prayer life—a worship life, a devotional life, a life already set apart for the Lord. This angel did not just walk up on any old girl in Nazareth. The bible says the angel was sent specifically to a Nazareth virgin named Mary, the one who was engaged to a man named Joseph. So I submit that Mary was able to WAIT, because she had an ongoing relationship with the one true and living God.

Listen, I don't see in the text where Mary was forced to say yes, do you? I don't see anywhere in the scripture that Mary was in a trance or put in a deep sleep like Adam, when God needed his rib to make Eve. Mary wasn't cast out on the Isle of Patmos like John the Revelator when she heard from God. She was not in turmoil running from God's will like Jonah in the belly of the whale. When God got Mary's attention, she was fully conscious, fully aware of what was going on in her life. She must have been listening intently to when the angel spoke and she seemed to know her whole world was being changed when she said, *Yes Lord*!

I don't know about you but God's will is what I want! I am the Lord's servant, and I too am willing to accept whatever God wants. Contrary to what some brides might think, Mary had not lost her mind when she said *Yes* to something that might have sounded so unbelievable to others—put your plans on the back burner and become the mother of the son of God. Oh, yes, Mary had a relationship with God; she had faith and trust in Him. Mary had obviously learned how to wait on God's will for her life. So she was the vessel God knew He could use for His *divine assignment*!

As a willing and waiting vessel Mary certainly didn't seem startled with the angel Gabriel appeared and said, *Greetings, favored woman*! *The Lord is with you*! But there's something else that many people tend to miss in the story in St. Luke. When the angel appeared it soon became apparent that it was not just Mary but Mary and Joseph who would have their life turned totally around as *Vessels of God*. There would have been real desperation caused by God if He had not had a willing couple of vessels. Both names are called in the bible because it would take both of Mary and Joseph them to complete God's *divine assignment*. God knew that Mary was engaged to Joseph. And God intended for Jesus to have both an earthly mother and father. The angel was not sent to break this couple up. God sent the angel to both Mary and Joseph because they were a team. And both she and Joseph already had established relationships with God.

You might recall that in the Gospel of Matthew, the Lord spoke to Joseph in a dream and assured him that the child Mary was carrying was indeed the Son of God—and that Mary had not been unfaithful to him. The Lord told Joseph not to put Mary away, but to marry her—and Joseph obeyed. I know that Joseph knew God for himself because Joseph too had plans for a special wedding and a special life with Mary. So Joseph helped to fulfill God's *divine assignment* and married Mary, right away. Joseph who had decided to put Mary away privately and call off the wedding, in the end, set aside his fleshly pride. Before he did you could almost hear him thinking with his ego and saying, *Here, I've been waiting all this time, keeping myself for this woman, not demanding a sexually intimate relationship with her although we are already considered to be married, and she turns up pregnant by another man.*

That was flesh talk! But I know that this man that Mary was engaged to marry and spend the rest of her life with was a man of God—because as soon as God spoke to him, in a dream, Joseph too obeyed. Mary and Joseph were on one accord, spiritually! They both, in effect, said the same thing to God, *I am the Lord's servant and I am willing to accept whatever He wants. May everything you have said come true.* What a strong message for folks desiring marriage. You need to make sure you and your partner are on one accord spiritually or you will never be able to truly fulfill the will of God for your lives.

The final reason that I believe God chose Mary as a vessel for His *divine assignment* is because Mary was also a *Worthy Vessel.* Mary, in other words, had all of the three W's for a *divine assignment.* She was a *Willing, Waiting, and Worthy Vessel.* How do I know? Well, after reading that an angel was sent to a Virgin named Mary, it struck me that God chose Mary because she was a *usable* vessel. She was a virgin—symbolizing that she was clean, untainted, unblemished. A virgin! Untouched! But I believe there's more to the story. You see, virgin also meant young. Therefore, Mary was pure in mind and body.

She was empty so to speak. Life had not filled her up to the point that she could not receive the pure things of God—the Holy things of God, the sanctified things of God. A virgin in essence was just the right vessel with room to receive a new vision; a vessel with room to receive God's purpose. Have you ever heard of people being set in their ways? I've heard women and men say, "I've been by myself so long I don't know if I can live with anyone. I'm accustomed to doing things a certain way—what if he leaves the cap off the toothpaste? What if she wants the side of the bed I'm accustomed to sleeping on?" All of that is called—being set in your ways, not willing to change. It's not being open to new things; wanting things to remain the same.

No wonder God can't use some of us as vessels—we're already too full! We're too full of self-will, too full of fear. Too full of doubt! Too full of unbelief! Too full of, "I've always done it this way." Yes, we're too full for God to pour a divine assignment into our lives. We're too full for God to do a new thing in our lives. Too full for God to use us! Our vessel is just too full!

But not Mary. Mary says , *I am the Lord's servant. And I am willing to accept whatever he wants. May everything you have said come true.* God was not the cause of Mary's desperation or problems. She would soon have joy because she had proven to be a willing, waiting, and worthy vessel. And God will not be the cause of your desperation when you remember to say, *Thy will be done*! We can all be vessels that God can use to get glory and honor out of, but we too must be *willing* and *worthy* of divine assignments. DON'T LET THE NIGHT BEAT YOU!

KNOW HOW TO CONQUER YOUR JERICHO!

You too will have A DIFFERENT SPIRIT when you know that FAITH MAKES THE DIFFERENCE! Oh, yes TRUST AND OBEY. Go ahead, holler out: LORD, HELP ME TO HOLD OUT! Be A CHOSEN VESSEL like Joseph.

Don't let GOD BE THE CAUSE OF YOUR DESPERATION! PRAY, now! PRAY, everyday! PRAY for me, for you, for others! Sing unto the Lord with a joyful heart!

Sing and pray your way out of desperation. You know the words...*Lord, you are the Potter*!

USE ME, MOLD ME, HAVE THY WAY, LORD!
HAVE THY WILL!

WHEN GOD IS THE CAUSE OF YOUR DESPERATION
St. Luke 1:26-45

STUDY QUESTIONS

1. What you have a personal relationship with God like Mary had the source of your desperation is not God. When was the last time you felt desperate? Were you moving toward or away from God? What were the consequences of your desperation?

2. What kind of health is your vessel in? What do you fill it with on a daily basis?

3. What prompted the virgin Mary to say so quickly that she would obey God?

4. According to the message in this chapter, what are the three characteristics of being a chosen vessel?

5. What evidence is there in the bible and in this chapter that Joseph and Mary were both chosen vessels?

6. What does it mean to say that God *can cause* desperation?

CHAPTER XV

A CHOSEN VESSEL
SOMETHING ABOUT JOSEPH

St. Matthew 1:18-21

Now the birth of Jesus Christ was on this wise: When as his mother Mary was espoused to Joseph, before they came together, she was found with child of the Holy Ghost. 19 Then Joseph her husband, being a just man, and not willing to make her a public example, was minded to put her away privily. 20 But while he thought on these things, behold, the angel of the Lord appeared unto him in a dream, saying, Joseph, thou son of David, fear not to take unto thee Mary thy wife: for that which is conceived in her is of the Holy Ghost. 21 And she shall bring forth a son, and thou shalt call his name JESUS: for he shall save his people from their sins.

Although some may not realize it, Joseph's role was just as important in the miraculous birth of Jesus Christ as Mary's. And I would submit that both Mary and Joseph had a personal relationship with God before they even knew they were to become chosen vessels for a DIVINE ASSIGNMENT!

But to understand Joseph's role let's first recall what happened to Mary when the angel appeared so that we can put the reflections in this chapter in context. According to *The Holy Bible,* we are all vessels—some of honor and some of dishonor. Paul knew this when he wrote in 2 Timothy 20:21, 22 that, *If a man therefore purges himself from these, he shall be a vessel unto honor, sanctified, and meet for the master's use, and prepared unto every good work. Flee also youthful lusts, but follow righteousness, faith, charity, peace, with them that call on the Lord out of a pure* heart. Oh, yes, there are indeed vessels of honor and vessels of dishonor.

We also learn from our scriptural readings that God needed a human vessel—a vessel of honor—to bear God's only son, so that the Jesus would be both *human* and *divine.* But did you know that God's chosen vessel did not audition for the part? Mary's name was not chosen out of a lottery. She certainly was not the only virgin in the land during her time. But, God chose Mary! God favored Mary! He saw something in Mary that pleased him above all others. And that's why God sent the angel Gabriel to tell Mary, *You are highly favored among women.* Now forget about being jealous of Mary or of what God does with other vessels. The vessels have nothing to do with it! All they know is that God favors them.

And, no matter how jealous of them you become, how envious, how critical, how better qualified you think you are— you can't change what God decides to do. And listen carefully, especially if you wish you were chosen. It's not about you. It's about God. His decision to favor and use whomever He chooses for His divine purposes is all it's about. Tell yourself, right now, WHAT GOD HAS FOR ME IS REAL!

You know the Christmas story, don't you? The angel spoke to Mary, told her that the Holy Spirit would overshadow her and that she would become pregnant. Then the angel told Mary, oh by the way, you're going to have a son and call him Jesus. Now you might be wondering, at least is you didn't read the last chapter, why God choose Mary, a virgin girl from Nazareth, to carry out such an important assignment. Stop wondering. You'll never fully know the mind of God; God's thoughts are *not* our thoughts. God's ways are *not* our ways!

What we do know is that, first of all, God found Mary to be a *Willing Vessel.* She must have been because when the virgin Mary heard the angel's message from God, she said, *I am the Lord's Servant, be it unto me according to your word.* Now, that's the language of a *willing vessel,* isn't it? Would you have responded like that? No, some of us would pick and choose where and when we would be of use to the Lord. Some of us think some assignments are too meager for our status and others would have to have totally logical explanations for what God is about to do. No wonder it is hard to be a willing vessel—we think it's all about us. Too many of us seem to forget that it is not about us, but about God. It's about His kingdom, not ours.

Of course, Mary and Joseph had plans; they were going to get married and do things together. Yet, Joseph, as well as, Mary was willing to set aside what they had planned on. And that's a good thing because neither could have gone forth without the other. Mary was not desperate to marry Joseph; Joseph was not desperate to marry Mary. But they were both desperate not to disobey God. Something about Joseph and not just Mary made them chosen vessels together. Joseph did not turn his back on Mary. He did not cause God to create a desperate situation in his life to get his attention. Oh, no. Joseph trusted God, even in a dream when God told him to stay with Mary even though the virgin was pregnant. "Pregnant with what? With whose child?" Joseph might have asked. But as a chosen vessel, he didn't. He took God at his Word. And I contend that, just like Mary, God knew that Joseph also was a willing, waiting, and worthy vessel.

Joseph trusted the Lord so much that he shared his only begotten wife-to-be back with the world. For Joseph obviously had learned that *the way up* and and *the way out* of anything or any situation is having a personal relationship with God.

SOMETHING ABOUT JOSEPH made him know that being a worthy vessel meant having faith and trust in God.

He was indeed, A CHOSEN VESSEL!

What's keeping you from being one, too?

Be A CHOSEN VESSEL! Be willing! Be worthy!

A CHOSEN VESSEL
SOMETHING ABOUT JOSEPH
St. Matthew 1:18-25

STUDY QUESTIONS

1. What three characteristics make Mary and Joseph chosen vessels?

2. Read all of St. Matthew 1 about the birth of Christ to answer the following three questions: How many generations are there from Abraham to David? What is another name for Jesus? What does it mean?

3. What did Joseph do after being raised from sleep?

4. Recall a time when you have been desperate to leave someone or marry someone or change a situation. To what extent did the outcome move you closer or farther away from God?

5. Why is understanding Joseph's role in the birth of Jesus useful for understanding the Christian walk?

6. Which of the twenty-five verses in the first chapter of St. Matthew are you most likely to memorize or remember?

CHAPTER XVI

IMPOSSIBLE THINGS ARE HAPPENING EVERYDAY

St. Luke 1: 37
For with God nothing shall be impossible.

This is the story of Zacharias the priest and his wife Elizabeth, both righteous before God, walking in all the commandments and ordinances of the Lord, blameless. They had no children because Elizabeth was barren and now they were both stricken in years. It was not Zacharias' time to burn incense when he went into the temple of the Lord. And the bible said that a whole multitude of people were praying without at the time of incense.

And there appeared unto Zacharias an angel of the Lord standing on the right side of the altar of incense. And when Zacharias saw him he was troubled and fear fell upon him. The angel tells him 'fear not' for thy prayer is heard and your wife Elizabeth shall bear you a son, and you shall call his name John. You shall have joy and gladness and many shall rejoice at his birth. And the angel went on to tell him all the wonderful things this child would grow up and perform in the name of the Lord. *Mainly, He shall go before the Lord and make ready the people to receive the Lord.* And the bible said Zacharias was terrified!

Now let me say this, Zacharias is a classic example of most Christian's reaction to a miracle. The Lord sends a message of hope, of increase, of advancement, of prayers answered, of dreams come true. And even though we claim we are people of faith, we are quick to speak of doubt.

The Bible said that after the angel told Zacharias all these wonderful things, Zacharias said to the angel, *how shall I know that this is so, for I am an old man and my wife is getting on in years?'* Can you hear the doubt? The angel told the doubting Zacharias the source of his authority by saying, *I am Gabriel, I stand in the presence of God. I have been sent to speak to you and to bring you this good news.* Even though Zacharias's prayers were answered, he lacked faith. Gabriel knew that immediately and said, *But now because you do not believe my words which will be fulfilled in their time you will become mute, unable to speak, until the day these things occur.*

What a price to pay! But church, there are always consequence to doubting God's word. That's why so many of us are not where we could be today. There's too much doubt in our spirits. There's even doubt in our actions in and out of church.

Now realize that it was just six months later that the bible tells us that the same angel goes to a virgin named Mary and tells her that she is to become the mother of the Messiah. On hearing this, the virgin said, *How can this be, seeing I have not known a man.* And Gabriel, the angel, explained that the Holy Spirit would over shadow her and that she would become pregnant with a child that she would name Jesus because *he would save his people from their sins.*

Now why the difference? Why was Zacharias struck dumb and Mary given an explanation? Certainly both events reflect that IMPOSSIBLE THINGS HAPPEN. In my earlier days reading the bible I thought that it was because Zacharias answered in doubt and not with faith. But later I saw that the answer goes even deeper than that. Now it seems clearer to me. The angel reacted harshly toward Zacharias because God expects more from a Priest, a man of God who has devoted his life to serving God. Zacharias being a priest symbolized maturity, spiritual growth, and strong faith in God. Certainly he should have known by then that with God all things are possible.

And perhaps there's a lesson there for us, also. It may well be that the angel's hard response to Zacharias means that God expects us *to expect* something from him. God expects us to expect great things because we serve a great God! As servants of the Most High God, we would do well to remember that we are standing and serving on Holy Ground! When we are on holy ground, any thing is possible—healing, deliverance, salvation, proclamation; it's all possible on Holy Ground. Every servant in God's house should be on his or her post *and* expecting a miracle; expecting God to show up at any second!

So wake Up! Sit up. Stand up! Be on guard! Be on your watch. Be available. Free your mind. Free your hands. Free your spirit. God is getting ready to do a new thing. When you're standing in a sanctuary or elsewhere on Holy Ground you should be ready for the Lord to *show up* and *show out*! Why? Because at some point, God wants to see our Faith In Action. He wants to see our walk, not just our talk. God expects us to become mature Christians; Christians who will take God at God's word! Our faith ought to be maturing with service. And what you couldn't believe God for last year, is a piece of cake this year, because you have matured in faith. Yes, we ought to have a stronger personal testimony in 2004 than we had in 2003 or 2003. We ought to have a stronger one in 2008 than in 2007 or 2005. And we ought to have our feet on the Head of some of those devils that have been taunting us.

Listen, little baby Christians ought to be the only ones still whining and stumbling around making the same mistakes, over and over again. Mature Christians won't be whining because by now they know how to STAND. Mature Christians know that we are not called to be mountain climbers, but *mountain movers*. Mature Christians are not afraid of the enemy—you don't have to run from the enemy. Speak to the enemy. Tell the enemy, *Get thee behind me, satan! Get thee behind me, satan!* Say it again, louder. Resist him and he will flee. Mature Christians ought have TONGUE POWER! Speak to the mountains in your life and demand that they MOVE!

Speak to your low self-esteem and tell it, *I am fearfully and wonderfully made.* Speak to those things that are NOT, as if they *were.* Act as if you believe God. I don't care what it looks like, say to yourself, *I believe God!*

Oh, yes! God is looking for a mature faith at some point in our Christian walk. The bible says that *by faith, the elders obtained a good report.* It is not our works, it is not our deeds. It is our faith that counts with God! Look at Elizabeth in the bible and see a crucial lesson in faith. She shows that it is not always the one in high office who has greatest faith. We like to think that the pope or the High Priest or the Bishop or Pastor has all the faith in the world. But be careful because it's not necessarily so! The widow who gave her very last dime. The lad with two fish and five barley loaves—Honey, now that's real faith! It's not always the glamorous folk in church. Sometimes it's that little grandmother on the last row with no office or title and no position in the church that has more faith in her little finger than the entire Board of Deacons or Stewards or Bishops.

Aw-aw-aw, she has that mountain moving faith. The kind that has helped her to make it this far. That's how she raised her family, that's why she can pay tithes faithfully on a fixed income when others with excess money cannot bring tithes consistently. Her faith is what keeps her praising God, in season and out of season. She never went to Seminary, has no degrees, but great faith. She has the kind of faith that says, *The Lord will make a way Somehow!*

Go back and read the first chapter of St. Luke. You will see that it wasn't Zacharias, the Priest, that demonstrated strong faith. It was Elizabeth, the woman who was once barren. When she got the news that her barrenness had come to an end, she said, *The Lord has done this for me! In these days he has shown his favour and taken away my disgrace among the people. He did this for me in my old age!* In those days, every Jewish woman wanted to give her husband at least one son. And apparently Elizabeth had kept on saying her prayers, year after year after year. At 18…then when she was 20 years old, then 30,

40, 50, 60. Still no baby, but she kept praying. Folk thought she was crazy, but she kept praying. Folks thought she was mad, but she kept expecting. We should do the same; keep believing God for the impossible because IMPOSSIBLE THINGS HAPPEN EVERYDAY.

So when Elizabeth conceived in her old age—way past childbearing age—she immediately gave God the praise. We don't hear her cursing God because she had to wait so long! We didn't hear her doubting God or going to the doctor to get a second opinion. No, she said look what the Lord has done for me! While Zacharias, the Priest, was asking HOW, Elizabeth was saying, thank you! While Zacharias was doubting, Elizabeth was rejoicing! Somebody reading this or hearing this, ought to take a lesson from Elizabeth—keep praying! Keep saying your prayers because miracles happen. Keep on trusting, keep on serving, keep on hoping because IIMPOSSIBLE THINGS ARE HAPPENING EVERYDAY.

Now that's the good news—with God, nothing shall be impossible unto you. If you truly believe God, your first name ought to be FAITH and your middle name HOPE! Every time you open your mouth you ought be saying, "I sure HOPE so! I BELIEVE so. You should be saying, *God said it, I believe it...IT IS SO*!!! And there's power in a whole congregation saying IT IS SO! That is how our Mt. Calvary African Methodist Episcopal Church in Towson, Maryland successfully did the impossible— together we *paid off a fifteen-year million dollar plus mortgage in five short years*! We spoke it into existence before anything ever happened. When we didn't have two nickels to rub together, we walked around daily saying—IT IS SO! And guess what? One Christmas Eve without ever having had bake sales or other types of fundraisers, our faith became Sight! Because we believed as a congregation that IMPOSSIBLE THINGS ARE HAPPENING EVERYDAY, they did. Suddenly, people around the nation and the world heard about what faith did at a little church on the east side of Towson near Baltimore.

Believe me, FAITH MAKES THE DIFFERENCE! You may be 30, 40, or 50 but you can still finish school. You may be 65 or 78, but you can still lift some weights or walk around the block. I know you've been in every drug program in the state, but you can still be delivered. I know you tried and your marriage failed but, give it another shot. I know you fail the Bar Exam or the Medical Boards, the SAT's or the law school exam, but keep the faith, try again. Desperate people do desperate things when a loan is denied, the mortgage is foreclosed, or a job is lost right at Christmas time. Your loved one died and you don't know how you are going to make it. Been there, done that you say?

Well, hold up! These kinds of things mean that we need to learn to EXPECT THE IMPOSSIBLE! Remember what the angel told Mary about her cousin Elizabeth who was called barren? In the sixth month the angel Gabriel was sent to tell Mary, the virgin, she was pregnant and Elizabeth hid herself five months after she learned in her old age that she was pregnant and no longer barren. Elizabeth was barren most of her life but kept on praying for a child. So the message for you is just keep on hoping, keep on expecting, keeping on believing! Keep on saying your prayers because we are not going by what we see or by what they call us, but by what the Word of God says.

I don't know about you, but I'm going to become pregnant every chance I get—PREGNANT WITH POSSIBILITIES. I am going to become PREGNANT WITH HOPE. I'm always just right for a miracle because I believe God. IMPOSSIBLE THINGS ARE HAPPENING EVERYDAY, have you noticed? In case you haven't I am here to remind you that Jesus Christ of Nazareth was born to bring us out of darkness and into His marvelous Light. Look around you. No matter where you live you're surrounded by darkness. The headlines and news programs tell daily of murders, rapes, hostage takings, innocent children being shot sitting in their homes, mothers and fathers killing their own children. Too many of us are aware of children selling drugs in schools and taking money home to a mother with a cocaine habit herself. We live in cities full of darkness.

These are desperate times and desperate people are praying desperate prayers. Where are you looking for relief. The news tells us there's corruption in high places; the police are often more corrupt than the people they arrest. The mayor walks around with blinders on and not admitting that things are not getting better, but telling us to BELIEVE. Believe What? School teachers and administrators are being fired by the hundreds. Some even report they are being paid for doing nothing. In the City of Baltimore the schools look like a war zone, yet, our children are expected to learn something in them. Black on Black crime has not declined and even though there are churches of nearly every denomination on virtually every corner in Baltimore City, thousands upon thousands of people of all ages go unsaved. They don't know what it means to have a personal relationship with the God that makes the impossible, possible.

We need more young Black men who live above the fray. Men like a young minister named Anthony Chandler. How did he come to be married to a *saved* woman and have three beautiful children. How come he's not just being "*my baby's daddy?*" Why isn't this young, good looking man out chasing women? When many Black men his age have yet to finish high school, what explains his motivation for completing college, attending seminary school, and earning a Doctorate in Ministry degree by the time he had turned 30. What does an Anthony Candler have that hundreds of other young men in the neighborhood where he was raised do not have? The answer is as plain as the nose on my face: Anthony Chandler has an abiding faith in his God. He chooses to believe God. He expects miracles and he gets them. He's a willing vessel who shows that he has a different kind of spirit. When asked why and how he made it, Anthony Chandler simply says: *I am what God says I am.*

Listen, the point is, don't let your culture define you! Let God's Word define who you are. The impossible happened with Elizabeth; it can happen with you. Known throughout her village for decades as an old barren woman, God changed her image and her identity. Just by telling her that she would bear a son, God showed what praying can do. That tells me that it doesn't matter what I was yesterday; it doesn't matter what you were. Our God is a present tense God. It doesn't even matter what a situation looks like. If God says it is so, it is so. Expect the impossible! Are you what He says you are or what you say you are? Low self-esteem? Hurting? Look to God not to some other human for recovery. No one has the last word on you or me, but Jesus.

So call me righteous, call me saved! And while you're at it, call me VICTORIOUS; call me healed and filled with the Holy Ghost. I am indeed more than a conqueror. Call me his servant! Call me delivered, liberated, sanctified. I am God's Prophet. Call me Fruitful. Call me the redeemed of the Lord. Now, you can call me, a little Black girl from the projects of Raleigh N.C. or Doctor Ann...*I am what He says I am!* Why? Because I am! How? Because with God all things are possible. But if you don't know that you will stay in a desperate state; you will pray desperate prayers. Wake up! It's time to see that IMPOSSIBLE THINGS ARE HAPPENING EVERYDAY when you trust and obey the lion of the tribe of Judah, the Lord of all, the author and finisher of our faith!

When your back is against the wall and you're feeling desperate take a closer look at your relationship with the Light of the World. Are you walking toward the light or away from it? God sent his son to make a difference; not just to save our souls, but to save our lives!

Expect a miracle and live like you expect impossible things to happen everyday. To believe or not to believe... now that's the question and the answer! *For with God nothing shall be impossible.* IMPOSSIBLE THINGS ARE HAPPENING...

IMPOSSIBLE THINGS ARE HAPPENING EVERYDAY
St. Luke 1:37

STUDY QUESTIONS

1. What does it mean to say that impossible things are happening everyday?

2. How have you been affected by two impossible things that happened in your life or in some one else's life?

3. Mary says in St. Luke 1:45 that her soul doth magnify the Lord. What is another way of saying that?

4. On which side of the altar of incense was the angel of the Lord standing when he appeared unto Zacharias?

5. What is the primary lesson we learn from Zacharias' behavior when he was told that his wife Elizabeth was expecting in her old age and no longer barren?

6. Are you more like Zacharias, Elizabeth, or Mary in your Christian walk? Why?

IMPOSSIBLE THINGS ARE HAPPENING EVERYDAY
St. Luke 1:37

STUDY QUESTIONS

7. If impossible things are happening everyday is it possible that possible things are also happening everyday? Which verse in St. Luke 1:1-50 supports your position?

8. According to the message in this chapter what is the difference between a matured Christian and a baby in the Christian walk?

9. What could be another title for the sermon in this chapter?

CHAPTER XVII

DESPERATE PEOPLE DO DESPERATE THINGS

Genesis 38:12-16

And in process of time the daughter of Shuah Judah's wife died; and Judah was comforted, and went up unto his sheepshearers to Timnath, he and his friend Hirah the Adullamite. 13 And it was told Tamar, saying Behold thy father-in-law goeth up to Timnath to shear his sheep. 14 And she put her widow's garments off from her, and covered her with a veil, and wrapped herself, and sat in an open place, which is by the way to Timnath; for she saw that Shelah was grown, and she was not given unto him to wife. 15 When Judah saw her, he thought her to be an harlot; because she had covered her face. And he turned unto her by the way, and said, Go to, I pray thee, let me come in unto thee; (for he knew not that she was his daughter-in-law.) 16 And she said, What wilt thou give me, that thou mayest come in unto me?

The word *desperate* means to have lost hope; suffering from extreme need or anxiety for something; a loss of hope, and surrender to despair. As a state of hopelessness, desperation often leads to rashness. Whether or not we are willing to admit it, we have probably all had desperate moments, desperate days or weeks, and even desperate seasons in our lives.

If you really want to understand desperate times and desperate people read the entire chapter of Genesis 38. This pericope of scripture describes the actions of a desperate woman named Tamar. Tamar was the daughter-in-law of Judah, one of the twelve sons of Jacob. Tamar was told to remain a widow at her father's house having lost her husband, a son of Judah. While waiting for another son to become of age, she became desperate.

Why Tamar Was Desperate

When a person is desperate, it is fairly safe to assume that someone or something drove them to desperation. Desperation generally comes as a result of something not going the way one wants things to go. The text clearly shows that Tamar was desperate because of her marital situation and because she had no children by any of her husbands. A careful reading of Genesis 38:1-30 will reveal some of the reasons for Tamar's desperation.

First, she was unfortunate in love. Twice, in her young life, Tamar had become a widow. The Bible said that both her husbands, Er and Onan, died not long after the marriages. You will agree that becoming a widow not once, but twice in a short period of time might drive one to desperation.

To make matters worse, Tamar's father-in-law, Judah, lied to her about giving her the youngest son, Shelah, to marry as soon as he was of age. The law of Moses provided that widows could marry any living brothers in order to carry the name of the man, and to carry on his inheritance. But it soon became clear to Tamar that Judah did not intend to give the youngest son to her to marry, and she began to take desperate actions.

Now, let us not judge Tamar too quickly. As a matter of fact, some of us will be able to identify with Tamar. Not only was Tamar unfortunate in love, she was probably lonely. And like most women, she needed to be a part of someone's life. But she also needed economic support. Traditionally, women went from the care of one man into the care of another—from the father to the husband. So marriage was a very important part of a woman's life during those times. Marriage was indeed attractive during these times because women generally owned no property and received none of the family inheritance.

But there is still yet another reason for Tamar's desperation. Her body clock was ticking and she wanted and needed to have children. For children would validate her as being a "real woman." It was tradition in her society that only worthwhile women produced children for their husbands. Tamar also needed children to carry on the family name. Tamar's desperation is easy to understand. Not only did she not have a living husband, it was obvious that she was about to be jilted out of the one she was promised. Shelah had now grown up and Judah had not mentioned a marriage between him and Tamar.

...for she saw that Shelah was grown,
and she was not given unto him to wife.
—Genesis 38:14

While these are all valid reasons for a woman to become desperate, I believe that Tamar was desperate because she did not put her trust in God. Tamar's greatest mistake was that she waited on Judah to fulfill her life, when she should have waited on God!

Desperate Actions Follow Desperation

Once Tamar decided to take matters into her own hands, she devised a scheme to get her needs met, one way or the other. When was the last time you or someone you know, did that? We're told that in Genesis 38:14 that Tamar took off her widow's clothing and put on the clothing of a prostitute after she heard that her father-in-law had gone to shear his sheep. By then she could see that although Shelah was grown, she had not received any word about a promised marriage between them.

It must have been desperation that caused Tamar to place herself in a position to be bought for favors. It had to be desperation that caused Tamar to become someone she was not—a prostitute. Her story is not really that much different from the experience of many men and women today.

When people are desperate for relationships or companionship or have low self-esteem, isn't the same thing done?

We disguise ourselves.

We pretend to have no standards.

We cover up our morals.

We forget that we are a peculiar people.

We forget that we are not to conform to this world, but to be transformed by the renewing of our minds. When we're desperate, we cover up our Christianity and put it on a shelf until it is convenient to live *holy* again.

Out of desperation, women put their pride aside and suffer abuse, both verbal and physical, for the sake of a relationship. one. Women and men often, out of desperation, put their common sense on the back burner, like Tamar or Queen Esther before she came to her senses and allowed God to use her.

Young and older women know how to do whatever is necessary to attract a man or keep after one until he is gotten. And we know how to do that, don't we? We redress ourselves; we take off our church clothes and wear that dress that is cut too low up top and too high on the bottom. And, of course, it's always too tight, when we describe it as *just right*! Genesis 38:14 tells us that Tamar put her widow's garments off and covered herself with a veil *and wrapped herself, and sat in an open place which is by the way to Timmath.* She was going to get what she wanted that day, one way or another. Desperate people do desperate things; desperate prayers leads to desperate actions.

When we become desperate, we become compromised, like Queen Esther in the bible. Esther wanted to be in the king's harem, so she changed her name from Hadassah to Esther. She wanted to fit in with the Persians. She denied who she was. She pretended to be somebody other than who God made her and what her family had raised her to become. She was a Jewish girl posing as a Persian hoping to become the wife of a foolish man who did not even appreciate his former wife, Queen Vashti. Esther only got to the throne because Queen Vashti spoke up for herself. She was there only because Vashti *would not* compromise herself. Vashti said, *take my crown, but you can't take my self-respect; take my crown, but I'll keep my dignity.*

Tamar shows us that disguise is not always simply of the exterior. This woman covered her outer self so that her father-in-law would not recognize her. But isn't it the inner disguise that is even more dangerous? Isn't it what is being done to the heart that really matters? Esther compromised—she disguised herself because she did not want to be recognized as a Jew. Tamar disguised herself because she was desperate and wanted to get what she thought she deserved. Both ended up becoming someone other than who they were. Esther walked like the foreigners, lived like the foreign women in the harem, and dressed like the foreigners. She ate like the foreigners. She did everything to hide her Jewish heritage, her true self from others.

But in the process, she hid *herself* from her own self. How can we tell? We know because when her cousin, Mordecai, called upon Esther to be God's woman *for such a time as this,* Esther had obviously forgotten who she was. She was too caught up in her own disguise to come to the rescue of the Jewish nation. So you see my Christian sisters and brothers, it is dangerous to disguise yourself and pretend to be what you are not! The danger is that once you get out there, it may not be so easy to come back to your *true* self.

Results of Tamar's Desperate Actions

Know this, there will always be consequences for acts of desperation. The deception is captured in Genesis 38:15,16 when Judah comes upon Tamar.

> *When Judah saw her, he thought her to be an harlot; because she had covered her face. 16 And he turned unto her by the way, and said, Go to, I pray thee: (for he knew not that she was his daughter in law.) And she*

*said, What wilt thou give me, that thou mayest come
in unto me?*

How many know that if you place yourself in a compromising
position, you can always find someone to meet your price? But
the price you may have to pay may be more than you bargained
for.

Tamar is a good example even for modern times of the
causes and consequences of desperate actions. Out of her
desperation, she became pregnant with twins by her father-in-
law, Judah. The mess Tamar found herself in is familiar even
today. You have only to watch soap operas, television, and hear
about what is going on in a neighborhood. Tamar who thought
she was desperate because she was twice widowed and childless
created even more desperation for herself. She had to live in
shame in a community where everybody knew that she did not
have a husband (and in that day, having a baby out of wedlock
was as acceptable as it seems to be today—even by our
churches). It was all quite disgraceful for Tamar, Judah, and all
concerned. By the way, our desperate actions always affect those
who love us.

Tamar and her family could not have had a happy home;
the community knew Tamar had done. Notice that the bible does
not say that Judah eventually gave her Shelah to marry or that
Judah loved her or married her. Rather, the bible says quite
pointedly that *Judah went in to her no more.* Tamar was
abandoned, widowed, and pregnant. Been there, done that,
anyone? Tamar and Judah ended up being miserable people. She
tricked him and won the battle. But in the end, she lost the war.
Tamar got revenge from Judah, but she did not get happiness.

But God was merciful unto Tamar. She gave birth to two
sons of the tribe of Judah but notice that neither of them was the
messiah. Yet, in St. Matthew, in spite of being a prostitute, she is
listed in the genealogy of Jesus as having two sons for Judah.

And Judah begat Phares and Zara of Thamar...

Wait On The lord

I cautioned us earlier not to judge Tamar too harshly, because Tamar's mistake is the mistake we make all too often. We may not have prostituted ourselves, but we have gone ahead of the Lord and tried to work out our lives on our own. Tamar did not have faith or patience to wait on God. By disguising herself and prostituting herself, she clearly moved ahead of God! Who knows what God might have done for her had she waited on God—had she been patient and had faith? Instead Tamar moved ahead of God and devised a devious plan to get what she wanted, *by any means necessary.* Sounds like you and me, doesn't it? Oh, how DESPERATE PEOPLE DO DESPERATE THINGS!

But look what can happen under similar circumstances when we are determined to be faithful to God. Ruth was also a young widow, stuck with her mother-in-law, Naomi. Naomi had no more sons, but Ruth was devoted and faithful to Naomi and said, *entreat me not to leave thee nor to return from following after thee.* Unlike Tamar, Ruth found a purpose for her life. She spent herself trying to help Naomi recover from the loss of her husband and her two sons. Ruth had lost a husband, too. Ruth was childless, too. But Ruth got a job gleaning in the fields of Boaz. She was prepared to work to take care of herself and her mother-in-law. Ruth waited on God, and God gave her *exceedingly abundantly more than she could ask or think.*

Wait on the Lord, my sisters and brothers! You are sometimes going to have desperate situations in this life! But don't let your desperate situations drive you into doing the wrong things!

Let your desperate situations drive you into the arms of the Lord, not away from him! Desperate times need a closer walk with Jesus. He is worthy to be PRAISED at all times!

Trust the Lord!

DESPERATE PEOPLE DO
DESPERATE THINGS
Genesis 38:12-16

STUDY QUESTIONS

1. Describe a situation where you were desperate and made a desperate decision. What were the consequences?

2. What are the differences and similarities among Judah, Zacharias, Ruth, Esther, and Tamar?

3. What is another name you could give for this sermon about desperate people? What specific passages in the Bible would you suggest using for a message about desperate times and/or desperate people?

4. What is the relationship between the 23rd Psalm and desperate actions?

5. Think of a time when you were determined to get your way, what three things did you do that increased or decreased your relationship with God?

6. In this space please indicate which three sermons in *Desperate People* have helped you the most and tell why?